FRUIT & VEGETABLE GARDENS

THE NATIONAL TRUST GUIDE TO THE PRODUCTIVE GARDEN

FRUIT & VEGETABLE GARDENS

THE NATIONAL TRUST GUIDE
TO THE PRODUCTIVE GARDEN

FRANCESCA GREENOAK

— SERIES EDITOR —

PENELOPE HOBHOUSE

PAVILION

Published in association with
THE NATIONAL TRUST
36 Queen Anne's Gate
London SW1H 9AS

First published in Great Britain in 1990 by
PAVILION BOOKS LIMITED
196 Shaftesbury Avenue, London WC2H 8JL

Text copyright © Francesca Greenoak
Photographic credits listed on page 110

Designed by Elizabeth Ayer

A CIP catalogue record for this book is
available from the British Library

ISBN 1 85145 252 4

Printed and bound in Italy by New Interlitho, Milan
10 9 8 7 6 5 4 3 2 1

For my Mother

CONTENTS

THE PRODUCTIVE TRADITION

A small neat Garden claims to be preferr'd
To those of larger Size with shabby Mien
Where nothing but disorder can be seen . . .

But every Beauty ceases when compar'd
With what we in the fragrant Orchard find.
Here Vegetable Life displays her charms
In radiant colours and in sprightly dress
The Summer's Queen unfolds her juicy stores
In such ambrosial fruits, all coverd (o'er)
With spangled rinds of purple and gold . . .

These Garden Plots can never fail to please
Which most abound with sweet and fragrant flowers
Where all the Fountains are with Torrents fed,
And all the Walls with painted Fruits are clad.
from The Country Seat *by Sir John Clerk of Penicuik, 1731*

The idea that garden produce can be decorative has not yet been fully re-integrated into the way we plan and use present-day gardens, though there are signs that change is on its way. All too often vegetables are banished to a distant and unlovely patch, while the fruit garden resembles a zoo with its frames and cages and wired and netted enclosures. Those plants which yield pleasant things to eat are generally stigmatized as plain and utilitarian. Yet what could be prettier than a 'Salad Bowl' lettuce, a 'Brant' grapevine ornamenting a wall, a bank of wild strawberries, or an apple tree such as 'Ribston Pippin' with its handsome fruit and its dark leaves with the pale undersides? Even rows of onions ripening in late summer or cockades of winter-standing leeks

A wall-trained cherry tree at Hope End. Morello cherries make productive and decorative use of walls with a northerly aspect, as also do 'Victoria' plums, 'Jargonelle' pears, and trained red currants.

are attractive if fitted into a design which shows them off effectively.

Long-standing preconceptions have played their part in hindering an appreciation of the beauty of fruits and vegetables. In the year this book was written, a newly published book about gardens showed an attractively patterned fruit garden with fan-trained wall fruit and neat rows of dwarf trees and bushes in four rectangular grassy areas – a picture which was slackly and inadequately captioned 'the utilitarian aspect of the garden'. At the same time, there are interesting developments in productive gardening: the advances and innovations of the organic movement have been received eagerly by a public nervous about agrochemicals; there is an increased awareness and appreciation of fruit, and a willingness to experiment with less well-known fruit and vegetables from other cultures, principally China and Japan, and from our own horticultural history.

It is now becoming fashionable once again to grow fruit and vegetables, and it was no surprise to find universal approbation of the productive cottage garden which won a gold medal and the award for the best garden in the Chelsea Show in the 1988 anniversary celebration year, with its happy association of fruit, salad vegetables, herbs and ornamental flowers.

Garden visiting is a national pastime, and with a high degree of interest in kitchen gardens, those open to the public attract considerable attention. One can examine herb gardens, orchards, potagers and old-style kitchen gardens, period restorations and modern innovations. An additional insight into the cultivation techniques of the past can be discovered in exhibitions of garden tools and accessories. One such exhibition opened in 1989 at the National Trust property at CLUMBER PARK, housed in the impressive long conservatory and the potting sheds. The Museum of Garden History in London at St. Mary-at-Lambeth also has an excellent permanent exhibition and the churchyard there (in which the famous Tradescants, father and son, explorers and gardeners to Robert Cecil and Charles I, are buried) has been made into a garden of plants of their period, including many that the Tradescants introduced to British gardens. It is interesting to see runner beans, originally appreciated as ornamental plants, flowering on the high brick wall of the museum garden.

Nor is kitchen gardening a mere spectator sport: gardeners all over Britain are experimenting for themselves on great estates and small plots. Prince Charles acknowledges that it was the old walled kitchen garden of his home in Gloucestershire that principally drew him to the place, and he takes an active part in planning and maintaining the potager which he made to a design by the Marchioness of Salisbury. At the other end of the scale, the Centre for Organic Gardening at Ryton has made a productive and pretty garden which would suit the modest dimensions of a small modern house.

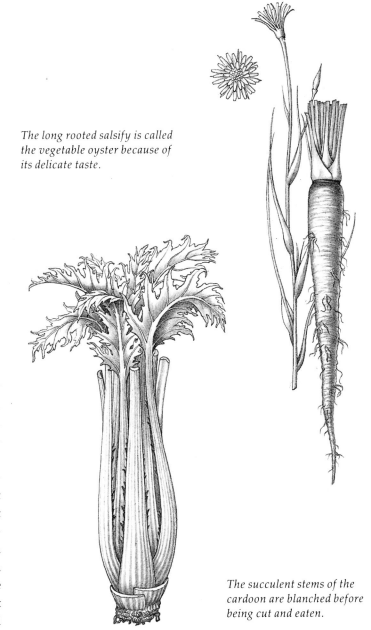

The long rooted salsify is called the vegetable oyster because of its delicate taste.

The succulent stems of the cardoon are blanched before being cut and eaten.

Two attractive old fashioned vegetables which enterprising gardeners are again growing in potagers.

*An attractive fruit walk at Erddig, with a neat gravel path. Wall trained apples to one side are
espaliered to five tiers, semi-dwarf apple trees grow on the other.*

The old apple trees at Lanhydrock in Cornwall include 'Bramley', 'Lord Derby', 'Newton Wonder' and 'Beauty of Bath'.

The modern kitchen garden has the advantage of scientific and technical knowledge, but takes many of its cues from the historic gardens. Fruit was viewed, in the past, as an important and demanding enterprise. It was not only that the kitchen garden was essential to the country estate for everyday produce, which could not always be reliably obtained elsewhere. The skills of the gardener could extend the seasons with a wide range of choice fruit and vegetables, and defy the limitations of the climate with carefully nurtured exotic plants which added variety to the diet. Good skilled gardeners were esteemed and sought after, and their work perceived as a valuable and creative contribution to the household. Nor was it considered beneath the dignity of even the proudest gentleman to take a positive practical interest in the doings of the garden.

For a seventeenth-century gardener such as William Lawson, fruit trees were not a routine drudgery of spraying and pruning, but a philosophical pursuit combining art and practical skills. The last chapter in his practical and influential book *A New Orchard and Garden*, which has been an inspiration to gardeners for over three hundred and fifty years, describes the way a well-disposed orchard 'makes all our senses swimme in pleasure, and that with infinite variety, joined with no less commodity'.

The pleasures of fruit and vegetable gardening have just as much a place in the context of present-day gardening; it is a matter of sharpening the senses to enjoy them. A head of prejudice seems to have built up against productive gardening, mainly on the grounds of the time it is believed to take up. I am continually asked how I manage to keep a fruit and vegetable garden alongside a demanding job and family responsibilities. Enquirers always overestimate the time I spend working in the garden; I don't think I am believed when I confess it usually amounts to the odd hour here or there, popped in when I can spare it. Moreover, it is insufficiently appreciated that growing food plants is a thoroughly satisfying activity and one which reaps great rewards for just a little skill and care.

It must surely be quicker and more efficient to go into the garden with a basket and pick a bowl of fruit, or pull some vegetables and gather some fresh herbs, than to go through the performance of driving the car out to the shops, to buy purchases several days old (which sadly applies even to vegetables organically grown for commercial purposes). Personally, I like the assurance that the vast quantities of fruit and vegetables my family and I consume are free from pesticide residues. Moreover, home-grown produce compares very favourably against the prices of organically grown goods in the shops.

For all its size and importance, the National Trust, like many a gardener of the present day, has a low staff to plant ratio. Because of this, fruit is more often a feature in their gardens than vegetables, although they hope to restore at least one fully working kitchen garden in the near future. Yet even when they are not working to full production, some of the great gardens of the past, conserved and restored, offer an insight into the attitudes and methods which were something more than utilitarian. Until the turn of the century, it was not unusual for large houses to have several orchards, fruit walks and a large kitchen garden. However, few private owners or organizations (including the National Trust) can now afford to garden on such a scale, and in the modern world ways have been found to make kitchen gardens reasonably practicable as well as productive. New techniques can be applied on large estates and by those with smaller gardens and only the labour of their own hands.

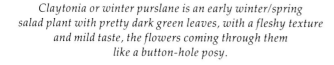

Claytonia or winter purslane is an early winter/spring salad plant with pretty dark green leaves, with a fleshy texture and mild taste, the flowers coming through them like a button-hole posy.

Land cress has a similar taste to water cress, though not quite so sharp. Summer sown plants are invaluable for winter salads, and like claytonia can be harvested leaf by leaf, or the whole head cut and left to regrow.

Innovating reformers, such as the Rev. J. S. Henslow (1796-1861) encouraged the poor of the rural villages to grow food for themselves on small plots of land. This idea was resisted strongly but ineffectually by local landowners around Henslow's home village of Hitcham in West Suffolk (from 1837), who believed it would give their working people too much independence. Henslow and other like-minded reformers also initiated village shows as a way of directing attention to growing and quality. However, before long the criteria for judgment began to concentrate on vegetables which were larger rather than of fine quality. Even in the nineteenth century this development had its critics. By 1885 William Robinson (better known for his works on flower gardens) translated the great French compendium of vegetables written by Vilmorin and Andrieux, prefacing it with the injunction that 'All who have gardens should fight against the deterioration of some of our best vegetables through the mania for size'. We have come almost to the end of the twentieth century before this good advice has begun to be heeded and yet there are still shows all over the country where size is the main criterion of merit – reaching its apotheosis in gargantuan but tasteless onions, leeks, beans and pumpkins.

Partly owing to the passion for size, gardeners in William Robinson's day as in our own tend to 'let things get old and hard before gathering so as to fill their baskets'. Many vegetables are spoiled, he noted, through not being picked at their tenderest stage: 'in Paris the cook has the upper hand and no grower dare send him the woody fibre which is so largely sent as vegetables to the London market.' When Raymond Blanc (of the restaurant Les Quat' Saisons in Great Milton) came to start his restaurant he found it impossible to convince gardeners that peas and beans should be picked young. During his early career in England, he took to raiding the vegetable patch illicitly by night, to outflank the implacable gardener. It is still difficult to find good vegetable products commercially, so the best thing to do is to grow them yourself – and enjoy the experience.

We have never had quite the regard of the French for their vegetables; there is as yet no garden corresponding to the famous seventeenth-century Potager du Roi at Versailles, a walled garden with twenty-nine separate enclosures within which all kinds of fruits and vegetables were grown, or to the accomplished early twentieth-century creation of the vegetable garden of Villandry near Tours in the style of a potager of the mid-sixteenth century. There are, however, several good gardens which offer models of various kinds to the British gardener.

Mrs Rosemary Verey at Barnsley House in Gloucestershire has made her own interpretation of the Villandry garden, now justly famous in its own right as a decorative, witty and productive English potager. UPTON HOUSE is one of the largest vegetable gardens of the National Trust, a traditional garden tucked into the hillside of a Warwickshire parkland. At Styal in Cheshire, the APPRENTICE HOUSE GARDEN shows an example of early Victorian produce grown according to the methods of the time, and there are several examples of organic gardens, many of which took their cue from the Henry Doubleday Research Association, who have at last managed to convince gardeners that organic methods are an advance on standard practice and not a narrowly nostalgic way of thinking. Ways of cultivating our land which are sustainable and enhance the environment are now beginning to be understood almost as clearly by gardeners as by ecologists.

In response to a renewed interest in fruit growing, the National Trust has restored old orchards and planted many new ones, some of them with an historical or regional theme.

The beautiful kitchen garden at Upton lies on a steep slope with an extensive pool at the bottom, a splendid centrepiece edged with ornamental gardens including the famous Upton borders which sweep down one side. The garden is very fertile as a result of centuries of cultivation of a wide range of crops. Visually it is stunning, with neat rows of soft fruit and vegetables interspersed by large old fruit trees.

Above: The pear alley at Bateman's, designed by Rudyard Kipling. The fine old pears 'Winter Nelis',
'Doyenné du Comice' and 'Conference' are trained up the framework over the path to make a fruitful tunnel,
interspersed with flowering climbers. Plants that will tolerate shade line the beds: large leaved bergenias,
lily of the valley, arching Solomon's seal and lungwort. Left: An orchard scene at Hardwick Hall, looking up to the
Elizabethan house. Working beehives within the orchard ensure good pollination and crops on these well-grown trees.

In these orchards and fruit gardens, visitors can admire gnarled old trees many hundreds of years old, and see new varieties on modern rootstocks which come into bearing within two or three years of planting. We can see and admire, for example, the turn of the century pear-tree tunnel in Kipling's garden, BATEMAN'S, in East Sussex, ancient figs or new pyramid apples at FELBRIGG in Norfolk, and numerous examples of wall fruit such as delicate plums, apricots and peaches, and venerable orange and lemon trees in orangeries and conservatories.

An extra benefit of visiting gardens and estates where the house is also open is the dimension given by old pictures of the grounds in earlier times. Paintings of DUNHAM MASSEY in Cheshire for example, show the view of 1697 with its extensive vegetable gardens and neatly trained wall fruit on the south-facing walls, contrasting with the views painted by John Harris the Younger about 1751 which show a totally different design with the wall fruit banished, extensive woodland planting and formal ornamental planting surrounding the house. Sometimes artistic licence confuses the issue; the view from the south of UPTON HOUSE by Anthony Devis blurs the kitchen garden terraces (and incidentally shifts the small temple) to focus on the gentlemen skating on the pool within an extensive park, with the house situated on the hill behind (rather more distant on canvas than in fact). Photographs of the gardens taken over the last hundred years give equally interesting insights into the design and workings of the gardens. Upton has a splendid view taken in 1904 showing the quiet pool and the productive gardens. At CALKE ABBEY in Derbyshire, old photographs supply important evidence, which is being used to reconstruct the history of the gardens. The kitchen garden on this estate was vast, and the plan for restoration, in fact, gives this over to ornamental plants while the smaller physic garden will be the site for a new kitchen garden which will specialize in plants contemporary with the house.

We all of us have to design our gardens according to the land, labour and time available, and though we may lament the passing of the great old kitchen gardens, few of us have the resources to emulate history on this scale. At least we can be glad that places such as Upton exist as a great living museum, and adapt and modify the practices which we see there and in TRENGWAINTON, MOSELEY OLD HALL, HARDWICK and other exemplary specialist gardens to our own situation.

Nowadays the smallest garden or courtyard can have its own fruit trees and bushes or herb troughs and hanging baskets and with the re-introduction of deep-bed methods, it is possible to raise good quantities of vegetables in a small space. Even after the EEC rationalization of vegetable varieties which resulted in the prohibition of the sale of certain kinds, there is still a wide choice from large and specialist nurseries and seed companies. It is also possible to grow banned varieties obtained from the Henry Doubleday Research Association through a special arrangement, especially if you are prepared to become a 'seed guardian' as Mrs Pat Brittan has at the Apprentice House Garden at Styal.

Such seed guardians volunteer to raise rare varieties of vegetable, undertaking to let some of the crop run to seed. This is collected and returned to the seed bank at HDRA. Private gardeners as well as institutions take part in this scheme which demands a methodical approach and reasonable degree of horticultural skill, especially with vegetables which are apt to cross-pollinate.

The situation for fruit has actually improved over the last few years with unusual varieties becoming available more easily and such a large range of dwarfing and semi-dwarfing stocks that one now begins to fear for the standard full-size orchard tree. In fact, the choice is so wide that is is difficult for beginners to be sure of making the right choice for their particular situation, and it is here that the possibility of seeing the trees growing in gardens and orchards open to the public is so valuable.

A view of Dunham Massey house and park from the south-east by Adrian van Diest, painted about 1697. Note that all of the south-facing walls are regularly patterned with plants, most probably wall-trained fruit.

FRUITFUL ORNAMENT: THE TRAINED TREE

It is not natural for fruit trees to grow in two dimensions, but we have pruned and pinned them into a multiplicity of unusual and ornamental shapes for centuries. Sometimes this is done purely for decoration, as in the delightful fruit allées of old – tunnels of trained trees, pretty in blossom as well as in fruit, which are now being reproduced in modern gardens. Sometimes there is some practical benefit, too, such as saving space, growing a fruitful screen or utilizing the existing support of a wall. Open-grown espaliers can also make an attractive way of dividing a garden and dwarf trees and single-stem cordons enable the fruit enthusiast with a small plot to grow a wide range of varieties.

Wall fruit is one of the most beautiful and evocative of forms, attractive in leaf, blossom and fruit, and even when grey-boughed through the winter months – especially with snow upon it. Trained as an espalier or fan, tender fruit benefits from the shelter and the extra warmth of a wall. Using the heat of a south-facing wall, one can grow apricots and peaches in the south and pears and delicate plums in the northern counties. Even a high cold north wall can be ornamented with Victoria plum since its heavy laden boughs, apt to break in open-grown trees, can be conveniently sustained by the fan supports. A morello cherry which will also take a northerly aspect will race to a span of 5m/16ft and a height of 2m/6ft – more if you let it – in as little as five years.

Walls are a particularly good place for growing cherries,

Approaching its fine-flavoured ripeness during September, the apple 'Orleans Reinette' is trained as an espalier against the long wall at Westbury Court Garden.

the fruits most sought out by birds. Sparrows will strip a tree growing in the open before you have a chance to pick any fruit, but a simple 'net curtain' (of almost invisible Netlon or a similar plastic netting) over a wall tree, hung from nails at the top of the wall, will deter the birds without harming them. Fruit on walls is immensely decorative and although the plants do not produce as much fruit as open-grown trees of free form, this is a good way of achieving a range of fruit in a smaller garden.

There are several methods of training the trees (or the bushes, in the case of wall currants or gooseberries), some of which have been practised for centuries. Espaliers are trained up from a single trunk, with branches limited to those coming out at right angles, at regular intervals in a series of tiers. The word strictly refers both to a lattice-work frame on which the tree is trained, and the trained tree itself. It derives from the old Italian *spalla* meaning shoulder supports – hence a 'shouldered' tree. An espalier may be three, five, seven or more tiers high. Apples and pears are the most commonly espaliered fruit trees, but others (including purely ornamental species) can also be trained into this useful form.

The fan-trained tree is virtually self-explanatory, the branches radiating out in a flat fan from a low trunk. There are in fact several ways of achieving the fan shape, which in my opinion is a more difficult form for the amateur than the espalier. It is probably best to buy a young tree already fan-trained so that the main work after planting is to train it on. A well-trained fan from a good nurseryman is a work of art and should be treated with respect.

TRAINING AN ESPALIER

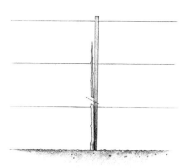

(a) Having erected the wire frame, plant a bare-rooted, maiden tree (unfeathered: ie without side branches) and cut the main stem back to about 50mm/2in above the wire, making sure there are three good buds showing near the top, the lower two facing outwards in opposite directions.

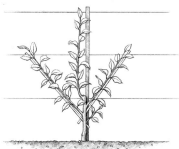

(b) As the shoots grow between spring and autumn the following year, train them gently but firmly up three canes fixed to the wires as shown, tying in the growth with soft string.

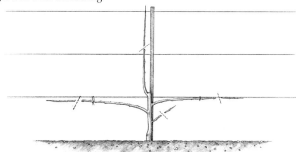

(c) After the leaves have dropped and growth halted (Nov-early Dec) bring the side branches down to the horizontal and tie them to the wire supports pruning weak new growth by up to a third. Cut back the upright branch to just above the second wire, making sure you have three good buds in roughly the right places and shorten the smaller side branches to three buds.

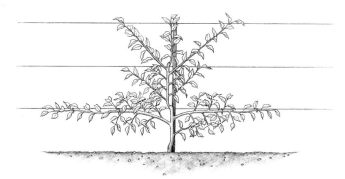

(d) During the following summer, train the second pair of branches in the same way as the first tier. In July-August, shorten growth from small branches growing from the main trunk, and branchlets growing from the two lower main arms to about three leaves (discounting the basal cluster).

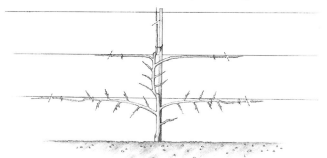

(e) In November, select two good outward pointing buds close to the third wire and cut the main upright leader back. Take the branches of the second tier down to the horizontal and prune these and the lower pair.

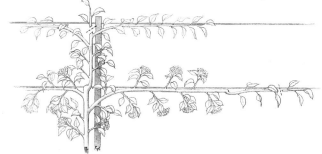

(f) Next season, repeat the procedure with the top pair of branches and cut the vertical trunk back to the top wire. As the branches all fill their space, cut back the ends of the branches each winter and prune the growth from the trunk and branches back to three leaves above the basal leaf cluster each May. Prune similarly later in the season to keep a neat shape.

A beautifully trained fan of a 'Wyken Pippin' apple inside the walled garden at Felbrigg Hall.
The other plants along this border are ornamentals, planted at a reasonable distance from the tree trunk and
bounded by a formal low box hedge.

One of the most handsome and best-flavoured culinary pears, 'Bellisime d'Hiver',
grown as an espalier at Westbury Court Garden. This variety, known in France since the seventeenth
century, has white flesh which keeps its pale colour when cooked.

Once espaliers and fan-trained trees have grown to maturity, the bamboos, wooden posts, poles and wires used for the initial training can be largely, or entirely, disposed of. The cordon, most commonly a single-stemmed tree with a stubby leaning shape, bears its fruit on short spurs coming from the trunk rather than branches. It is usually planted obliquely and needs supports all its life. This is not a method of growing to choose if you are a lazy pruner, for the tree constantly wants to outgrow its bushy leaning-tower shape, but it does provide an excellent way of concentrating a number of different varieties in a relatively small space.

Once the basic rules of pruning are learned, it is not difficult to keep wall trees looking nice, and it is by no means too ambitious for domestic gardeners to train them for themselves. It is however a sensible plan to look at some examples of wall fruit before making a decision about what fruit to choose and where to put it – moving a fruit tree is a much bigger enterprise than shifting a perennial planted in the wrong spot.

Many of the National Trust gardens have wall fruit, with fine examples at large gardens such as FELBRIGG HALL in Norfolk and in a smaller town garden such as the one at FENTON HOUSE in Hampstead. Restoration of the fabric of the walls in this London garden began in 1989 which entailed taking down the fruit, but there are plans to develop the fruit growing when the rebuilding is complete. One of the best displays is to be found at WESTBURY COURT in Gloucestershire, which has been restored from dereliction in the last two decades to resume something of its former glory as a William and Mary garden in the Anglo-Dutch style. Almost all the plants in the garden, including the fruit, are those which were known to have been grown about 1688. The great west wall, cut with three *clairvoyées*, which runs parallel to the long canal, has an impressive line of beautifully trained apples, pears and plums. Elsewhere in the garden every good stretch of wall (such as the outside surfaces of the walls of the small inner walled garden) is likely to have a small peach, apricot or plum upon it.

The appearance of the west wall gives you a good idea of why fruit ornamentation was so popular in the past. After nearly twenty years, the trees are in early maturity, stretching their boughs evenly against the brick and decorated with a froth of blossom in the spring. Swags of foliage, each variety slightly differing from the others in the greens of its leaves, hang the whole length of the wall in summer. In early autumn, the branches are clustered with apples in reds, russets, greens and orange-reds. 'Devonshire Quarrenden', which does particularly well, is crimson against dark green leaves. The 'Catshead' has a large oblong fruit knobbed near the eye and stem. 'Court Pendu Plat', the late-blossoming, late-maturing Wise Apple, good on heavy clay soils, has tiny bright red and yellow fruits.

Farther along the wall, apples give place to pears. The glossy foliage looks handsome in late summer, fluttering in the breeze against the fruits which ripen to green russet, yellow and dull crimson. There are famous names such as

An old English variety, the 'Catshead' apples have an unmistakable shouldered shape. 'Catsheads' are said to be the best variety for making dumplings.

'Jargonelle' and 'Catillac', 'Chaumontel' and 'Black Worcester' (said to be one of the legendary Warden pears). There are some grown in this garden that you will be unlikely to see anywhere else, such as 'Beurré Brown', which seems to have been introduced to Britain as early as 1550, and 'Forelle' with its beautiful, small well-shaped red fruits, crispy as an apple.

The Head Gardener Mr Kenneth Vaughan prefers espalier pears because they are easier to train than apples and they grow better but acknowledges that the display is mainly for ornament. Despite the inadequately drained, poor alluvial soil, the trees do well here and on the whole he leaves them to get on by themselves, whereas his counterpart of the seventeenth century would have had several under-gardeners working hard, looking for pests, thinning the fruits and watering throughout the summer. The received wisdom is that wall trees always require watering since rainfall does not always reach the base of a wall. The Westbury espaliers, planted extremely close to the wall, seem, however, to have found their own *modus vivendi*, which – if it does not maximize the fruit production – produces surprisingly good crops and minimizes labour, so reducing costs. Mr Vaughan believes that the roots, failing to receive water from above, have sought downwards for it.

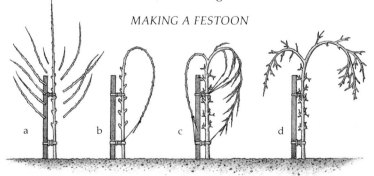

MAKING A FESTOON

(a) Shows a 1-year-old tree on Pixy rootstock on which all side shoots are cut to 3 buds in August. (b) Bend main stem over and tie it to base. (c) Second August: bend over and secure new shoots from leader, cut back others on main stem to 3 buds. (d) Third spring: untie festoon branches and trim main shoot to just below curve. Afterwards prune in summer to maintain shape and size. (If grown in a pot, choose 300mm/12in. Especially suitable for plum trees but not 'Victoria'.

Although the trees are not regularly sprayed against disease, they remain reasonably healthy. Research from the Ministry of Agriculture as long ago as 1982 showed that commercially grown apples would do just as well with a reduction of a third of the recommended spraying regime. In the context of a garden where there are numerous varieties, it is possible to manage without any pesticides. Not that Mr Vaughan is opposed to prophylactic pesticide spraying, it is 'simply a matter of finding the time'. In practice he treats problems 'as and when they occur – a systemic insecticide or general-purpose fungicide, directed towards a specific tree'. It is interesting to see that although all trees touched branches along the entire length of the wall, disease did not spread from one to another. Over the years, Mr Vaughan has observed, 'some individuals get canker, some aphids, some red spider – with a perfectly healthy and unaffected tree on either side'.

Even allowing that some trees are naturally more vigorous than others, the Westbury espaliers are superbly trained, but every once in a while there is an accident or a canker at the junction of branch and trunk and one of the shoulders loses its arm. In one place where this had happened, Mr Vaughan demonstrated how to cut away a very thin strip of the bark, just above the bud intended to start the new 'arm'. For this 'notching' procedure you need a very sharp knife and a steady hand. 'You have to go down to the white wood, and this encourages the bud to send out a shoot.'

Most of the open-grown fruit trees elsewhere at Westbury do well, but the morello cherries performed very poorly, especially in comparison with the vigorous gean or wild cherry trees. When they showed no sign of picking up, Mr Vaughan decided to take them out and replant morellos elsewhere as wall fruit, this being the usual way of growing this generally tolerant, north-wall variety.

This venerable espalier pear at Barrington
Court is a grey lace of old fruiting spurs and early
blossom in springtime.

Fruit trees can live to a venerable old age; some of the wall figs in the walled garden at FELBRIGG HALL are thought to be the ones first planted there. Tales of the 'white fig' and its prolific crops recur in old documents and records relating to the garden. In the 'exceedingly well-kept' kitchen garden, James Gigor (an early nineteenth-century visitor), remarked on the size and hardiness of 'the white Genoa Fig' (now called 'White Marseilles'), which he believed had been there well over a hundred years at the time he made his assessment, this kind of fig being noted for its 'extraordinary longevity'. In 1887, the Empress of Austro-Hungary, resting during a long journey, was 'regaled with figs from the walled garden'. The figs at Felbrigg continue to grow healthily on the warmest south-facing wall, sheltered by the other walls from the hard winds that sweep north Norfolk – and they still produce fruit.

In his review of this walled garden, Mr John Sales, the Chief Gardens Adviser to the National Trust, summarized:

'In the traditional way, there are fan-trained peaches, nectarines and gages on the south-facing walls, plums on the east-facing walls, and apple and pear espaliers facing west and south. Many of the older apples, some associated with East Anglia, are represented – 'Norfolk Beefing', 'Braddick's Nonpareil', 'D'Arcy Spice', 'Wyken Pippen', 'Ashmead's Kernel', 'Court Pendu Plat'. Here and there among the fruits, clematis and roses have been inter-spersed to give a touch of colour in summer.'

There are several old, full-sized trees in part of the ancient orchard section of the walled garden, but there are also a number of new dwarf-form trees. New plantings include the apple 'Norfolk Royal Russet' on MM106 stock which, trained into the modern pyramid form, comes into bearing only two

Top: 'Peregrine' peach is a good old variety for the English climate, growing ripe on the warm high wall at Felbrigg. Bottom: 'Wyken Pippin' apples ripen to a golden yellow and will last in store until February.

This alley of pleached pears at Beningbrough includes 'Pitmaston Duchess', 'Clapp's Favourite', 'Marie Louise', 'Easter Beurré', 'Beurré Hardy' and 'Black Worcester'.

Even though a season of growth may be lost, it is advisable for an intending fruit gardener to spend a period visiting gardens such as Westbury and Felbrigg, to look at the fruit. Catalogues from the famous fruit nurseries are very informative and many contain a surprisingly large repertoire, but it is unwise to make a choice simply from a description. Several nurseries now offer two hundred kinds of apple, and a large number of pears, cherries, plums and soft fruit. Most will give advice either by letter or telephone. Garden centres have gained a bad reputation for stocking only the popular lines in fruit, but it is well worth paying a visit to a local nursery. Very likely there is a local variety of fruit which is particularly well adapted to the local climate. Moreover, different varieties are better suited to one particular purpose than another, and by discussing one's choice with a nurseryman or gardener, one may avoid learning the hard way that certain very vigorous trees are not suitable as

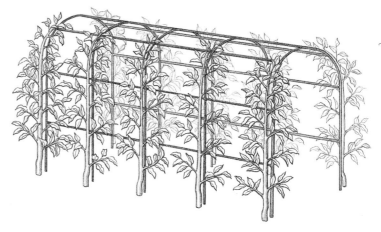

Above: Ready-made frames for fruit tunnels are now available from a number of suppliers. The trees planted on the outside of the frame are espaliered in pairs of the same variety.

or three years after planting. This is a small, easily pruned shape used usually for apples, pears and plums, where lower branches are longer than the upper ones, and which is usually grown to a maximum of about 2.5m/8ft.

wall or dwarf subjects or that some are more susceptible to disease. 'James Grieve' (rather prone to canker) is not, for example, an ideal subject for a heavily pruned form such as an espalier. It is also essential to have trees which are self-fertile or will pollinate each other. Generally speaking, this means ensuring that the varieties chosen have more or less concurrent flowering times (choose from the same group, or adjacent groups, in the chart below), but certain plums and cherries are fastidious about whom they will accept as a pollen partner. Most good catalogues and practical fruit guides contain pollination information.

Contrary to belief, some of the most famous fruits – 'Bramley's Seedling', 'Cox's Orange Pippin' and 'Discovery' apples and 'Victoria' plum to name just a few – were not the result of specialist breeding programmes, but chance seedlings, spotted by an observant gardener or nurseryman. There are many varieties which are locally renowned: 'Lane's Prince Albert' in Hertfordshire and 'Withington Welter',

---

APPLE POLLINATION GROUPS

A selection of well-flavoured varieties with their date of introduction and time of eating: groups are in flowering sequence.

GROUP 1 (flowering very early)
*Gravenstein 1669 *Sept-Dec.* Gold and red, fresh-tasting sweetish apples which will serve as dessert or culinary. Vigorous tree which grows well on dwarfing stock.

GROUP 2
Beauty of Bath 1864 *Early August.* Very early to ripen, small sweet juicy fruit. Tree partly tip-bearing.
Bismarck 1870 *Nov-Feb.* Large dark red cooking apple. Spreading tree, tip bearer.
Egremont Russet 1872 *Oct-Dec.* Delicious fruit with characteristic nutty, russet flavour. A good garden tree, growth neat and upright.
Irish Peach 1820 *Aug.* Fine-tasting early variety. A slender tree, of moderate growth, easy to cultivate.
Lord Lambourne 1923 *Oct-Nov.* Heavily cropping, compact tree. Fruit well-flavoured and sweet.
Margil 1750 *Oct-Jan.* Delicious fruit. Tree small and ornamental and not a heavy cropper.
*Ribston Pippin 1707 *Nov-Jan.* From Ribston Hall, Knaresborough. Beautiful fruit golden-brown, flushed red, with light russet. Rich sweet flavour.
Saint Edmund's Pippin 1875 *Sept-Oct.* Excellent early russet with characteristic flavour, ripening on compact, lightly spreading tree.

GROUP 3
Allington Pippin 1896 *Oct-Dec.* Self-fertile tree. Fruit can be eaten as sharpish dessert or cooking apple. Makes a large, vigorous, heavy-cropping tree.

*Belle de Boskoop 1856 *Feb-Mar.* Dual purpose medium sized apple, cooking well and good as dessert when fully ripened. Moderately large fertile tree (resistant to scab and canker).
*Blenheim Orange 1818 *Nov-Jan.* Famous dessert apple (can also be cooked). A fine, strong flat-crowned tree.
Discovery 1962 Fine-tasting, sparkling, early dessert apple, deep red with white flesh. An upright tree, resistant to scab.
James Grieve 1897 *Sept-Oct.* Eat sweet-fresh apples straight from the tree. Good in northern regions; grow in fertile soil to avoid canker.
Lane's Prince Albert 1857 *Nov-Feb.* Berkhamsted, Hertfordshire. Juicy sharp-tasting cooking apple, reliably fertile.
Rosemary Russet 1831 *Dec-Feb.* Handsome, fine flavoured apple for late-eating. Moderately sized tree, good as a half-standard in gardens.
Sturmer Pippin 1831 *Jan-April.* Excellent greeny apple with slight russet, which ripens late in store. Grows well on most soils, pick as late as possible.
Tower of Glamis 1750 *Nov-April.* Large culinary apple, green with a red brown flush. Tough, hardy tree.
Worcester Pearmain 1874 *Sept-Oct.* Good flavour when ripe, moderately large, fertile tree.

GROUP 4
Ashmead's Kernel c 1700 *Dec-March.* Aromatic, sweet, late-eating apple; tree of moderate size.
Cornish Gilliflower 1813 *Dec-Feb.* Best in a warm, wet climate such as that of its native Cornwall, where it makes a tree of slender growth. Best grown as bush or standard.

D'Arcy Spice 1848 *Dec-April.* Originated in Tolleshunt D'Arcy in Essex, and grows best in East Anglia. Delicious spicy apples, but not a strong or heavily cropping tree.
Orleans Reinette 1776 *Nov-Jan.* Exceptional flavour; large fruit on strong upright tree, but needs fertile soil or suffers from scab.
Tydeman's Late Orange 1949 *Dec-April.* Raised at East Malling, crisp, golden yellow apple, with sweet aromatic taste. Can slip to biennial cropping.

GROUP 5
Lord Derby 1862 *Nov-Dec.* Large green cooking apple with some resistance to scab and mildew, cropping regularly.
Newton Wonder 1887 Raised in Derby, a tall and spreading tree. Fruit cooks well and can be eaten as dessert apple in March.
*Gascoyne's Scarlet 1871 *Sept-Jan.* Brilliantly coloured apple, tree good on chalk soils and areas of late frost, vigorous, decorative but not heavy cropping.

GROUP 6
Court Pendu Plat (of great antiquity) *Dec-May.* Small apple, good rich flavour. Small hardy tree good on clay soils, does well in areas of late frost.

GROUP 7
Crawley Beauty 1906 *Dec-Feb.* Originated in a cottage garden in Surrey, a cold climate apple (scab resistant). Self-fertile, may be eaten raw or cooked.

* triploid, ie requires two pollen partners.

recently restored to the garden at Quarry Bank Mill APPREN-TICE HOUSE after much searching, both have such local historical associations and tend to do especially well in the soils where they originated.

For the private gardener, the advances in developing dwarf and semi-dwarfing rootstocks have made it possible to have several fruit trees in a space where there might barely have been room for one in the past. Few fruit trees are grown on their own roots, and while the job of grafting can be done by an amateur, it is usually carried out by the nursery professionals. Mr Ted Bullock, the Head Gardener at FEL-BRIGG, made whip-and-tongue grafts of special trees that he wanted to propagate (such as 'Old English Pearmain', 'Hubbard's Pearmain', 'Winter Majetin' and 'Striped Beef-ing') but in general, the Trust gardens order their trees from specialist nurseries, specifying the variety and rootstock according to the requirements of the situation in which they are to grow and the desired effect.

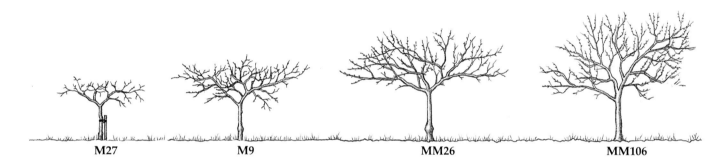

M27   M9   MM26   MM106

M27: A very dwarfing rootstock, for the small garden and for trees in tubs, stepovers and small espaliers in soil rather than grass. It rarely grows more than 2m/6ft in height or spread and crops soon after planting, but usually requires permanent staking and bare fertile soil.
M9: Dwarfing, producing trees around 3m/10ft in height and spread, it is usually grown as a bush tree with a permanent stake – much in use commercially but which requires careful pruning. Can be used for cordons, espaliers and fans in most soils.

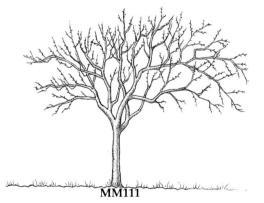

MM111

MM26: Semi-dwarfing, a little more vigorous than M9. Stakes can usually be removed after 5 years or so if the tree is strong, well-grown and reasonably sheltered from strong winds. Larger crops than M9.
MM106: Slightly more vigorous than M26, this is another useful stock which grows up to about 5m/16ft. It can be grown in turf when established and trained as a half-standard, large fan or espalier. It gives extra vigour on poor soils.
MM111: Vigorous, good for standards and half-standards, it makes large trees which crop well, but takes longer to come into cropping.

Apple rootstocks (guaranteed virus free) on which named varieties are grafted are known by their 'M' numbers. The choice of rootstock controls the rate of growth, the speed with which the trees will produce their first fruit, and the longevity of the tree (dwarfing stocks appear not to be as long-lived as large ones). It must be said that this is only a rough guide; the fertility of the soil, the climate and the natural vigour of the variety chosen also have an effect.

Modern rootstocks, unlike those of the past, are reliably standardized, and those certified EMLA stock (the initials taken from the two research institutions East Malling and Long Ashton) are guaranteed true to name and virus-free. Another advantage of these developments (especially to a private gardener who may face a move in a few years' time) is that the smaller trees come earlier into bearing.

An apple rootstock such as M27 will make a one-tier espalier or step-over tree (about 300mm/1ft high), or an open tree for a very small garden; the next size up, the M9 or M26 may be used for a slightly bigger tree, three-tier espalier or fan, and M106 will give a pyramid or a reasonably sized half-standard, that can reach up to about 5m/16ft or so in height and spread, maybe a bit more or less depending on the vigour of the apple variety chosen. M111 is the biggest and the most vigorous.

Pears are usually grown on quince rootstock; the smallest is Quince C which will give a mature tree of approximately 3m/10ft, and a strong espalier or fan. Pears on this rootstock will come into fruit more quickly than those on their own roots, but if there is space, it is a good thing to plant a natural full-size pear tree for its beauty alone. There is evidence to suggest that dwarfing rootstocks reduce the life of the trees, but a shapely full-grown pear (on pear rootstock) will certainly fulfil the saying, providing 'pears for your heirs' for a long time to come. Perry pears, widely planted by the National Trust, are grown on seedling pears for greater vigour.

At the other end of the scale, a recently developed rootstock called Pixy has made it possible for small gardens to accommodate delicious plums and gages which are only available if you grow them yourself. The more vigorous St Julien A is still used for fan-trained plums. The important thing to realize if you grow plums as wall fruit is that it is essential to prune them in late summer, no later than August,

The 'Williams Bon Chrétien' pears at Barrington Court in fruit. This delicious, musky-flavoured pear was raised by a schoolmaster in Berkshire a little before 1770, and has for many years been among the best-regarded of the early-ripening pears.

to reduce the danger of silverleaf disease. WESTBURY COURT has a nice range of very old plums and greengages grown as espaliers and fans.

Very dwarfing rootstocks have made it possible for fruit to be grown in pots or tubs: apples and plums can be grown as dwarf pyramids or looped over as festoons. Growing fruit in pots enables gardeners to experiment with fruit in harsher climates than would normally be possible, since plants may be brought into shelter in bad weather and through the winter. Pots also enable people to grow plants for which their normal soil is not suitable, so a chalky garden can have a blueberry in a pot of ericaceous compost, looking decorative as well as fruitful. Container-grown plants need extra attention, particularly watering, since they dry out very quickly. They also need regular liquid feeding and repotting about once every two years as well as careful pruning to keep them in trim.

In 1989, a tall columnar apple form made its public début at the Chelsea Show under the group name of 'Ballerina Trees' with three dessert varieties and a crab apple. In blossom they resemble garlanded poles. They were bred from a 'sport' (mutant) of a Canadian apple called 'McIntosh' and the new strain, which grew without branching, was known as 'Wijcik' (pronounced Wye-jack). Experimental work was carried out at East Malling Research Station in Kent, and while it was found not to have commercial value, it was developed into a new form for the gardening market. Unfortunately, the varieties which have so far been brought out in this form (the dessert apples 'Bolero', 'Polka' and 'Waltz') do not have a first-rate flavour but breeding developments may improve the future generations of columnar apples.

Time will tell how these apple-poles will thrive; they certainly provide an opportunity to grow several varieties in a restricted space, but they are expensive compared with the other single stem form, the cordon, while producing less fruit. This may be an innovation which remains a curiosity rather than a productive ornament.

ORCHARDS GREAT AND SMALL

In the past an orchard was considered a desirable or even necessary adjunct to the garden, but over the last few decades, the orchards in our landscape have been subjected to immense pressure for change. Commercial orchards have altered their aspect altogether with the heavily cropping trees on dwarf stocks taking the place of trees tall enough for one to walk beneath. Many orchards were grubbed up during a period of agricultural expansion, and in recent years others have found themselves under the greedy gaze of property developers.

A number of small orchards scattered about the Hertfordshire-Buckinghamshire border were planted by various members of the Rothschild family who built Tring Park, ASCOTT and WADDESDON. They were planted close to the workers' cottages, for the benefit of the staff who served the great houses and farms, from the overspill from the large Rothschild orchards. The land value of these half-acre orchards is now hugely out of proportion to that of the fruit produced by their tall, ageing, often neglected apple, pear and plum trees. Their aesthetic, historic and amenity value is incalculable.

Many small orchards such as these are now in the hands of private owners who inherited them with farms or found that house purchase included an orchard at the foot of the garden. The owners, recognizing the beauty and historical importance of these orchards, are often anxious to conserve them

'Autumn Golds' in one of the orchards at Hardwick Hall. The trees here are on a semi-dwarfing rootstock, but the effect is still one of peace and repose.

but uneasy as to how to proceed. Fortunately there is now a number of good examples of conserved and restored orchards, some of them owned by the National Trust, which has come over the past few years to appreciate their value and is fighting for their preservation.

Girton College, Cambridge was one of the first institutions to set a standard in orchard conservation. Adjacent to the college is the Old Orchard which was planted about the same time that the college was founded in the late nineteenth century. A second orchard was later established to the south of the college in 1948 as an addition to rather than a substitute for the Old Orchard. (Some of the fruit had won awards at RHS shows.) In 1980, the college formulated a structured approach to the conservation of old orchards, due to the foresight of a succession of head gardeners, in particular Mr Stephen Beasley who, alarmed to see that Cambridgeshire orchards had diminished from an area of nine hundred acres to three hundred acres in the thirty years up to 1980, determined to secure those at the college.

The Old Orchard, though indisputably past its prime, had played an integral part in the development and history of the college and continued to be an important amenity, a place where staff and students were encouraged to roam and enjoy the fruit. It also represented an 'example of a disappearing method of fruit production', both in the number of different cultivars represented within it and the fact that these were large standard trees. Some of these, the 'Blenheim Orange' for example, had been grown from the original tree at Woodstock; others are little-known varieties which could be an 'important source of propagating material for the future or used as germplasm for breeding programmes'. Old Orchard, like some of the ancient National Trust orchards, is in a sense a living museum, a reference point for identification, but it also uses the fruit it produces, the best of which goes to the college tables.

Both Girton orchards are now what commercial growers would term 'over mature' but they are productive enough for the requirements of the college which continues to propagate and plant new trees rather than grubbing up the whole orchard as is commercial practice. The new trees – mostly standards and half-standards, 'trees large enough for an undergraduate to lean against' – are interplanted among the old ones. This is the practice also at many of the Trust properties, where venerable and historic old trees have gaps between them left by the decease of their fellows.

At FELBRIGG HALL in Norfolk Ted Bullock has charge of a walled garden which is both productive and ornamental, in which there is a delightful orchard with flowering bulbs in the turf, and also herbs, flowering plants and vegetables. As at Girton, the older trees are now barely productive, but they add height and maturity to the orchard. Some of the first few new apple plantings (the Canadian variety 'Wellspur Delicious') did poorly, suffering, Mr Bullock surmised, from replant disease. Not very well understood as yet, this disease seems to affect new trees planted on ground from which old fruit trees have been taken out or where they have died, a problem of some significance when it occurs in an old orchard. The answer is to dig out a substantial quantity of soil and replace it with fresh soil and compost, or to choose the course taken by Mr Bullock, which was to sterilize the soil thoroughly in the planting area, using dazomet and covering the soil with polythene for two weeks, to seal in and retain the gas while the chemical took effect.

Ten new trees were purchased from a famous fruit nursery in 1980 on M26 stock, which is semi-dwarfing. Most of these were older varieties, and, planted in the orchard turf, at first they did not thrive. They grew more strongly when Mr

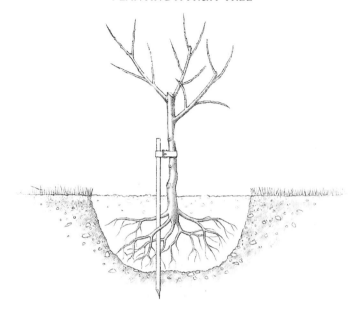

PLANTING A FRUIT TREE

It is most important to give a young tree a good planting hole, big enough (and more) to accommodate the roots fully extended. Fill the hole back with fertile topsoil, enriched with a handful of bonemeal. Position the stake securely before you plant the tree, then put the tree in so that the shadow on the trunk, indicating that it was below ground in the nursery is exactly at the same place with the soil level when planted. Firm down the soil as you plant so the tree is firm and secure but not compacted. Use a patent tree tie to fix it to the stake.

Bullock removed the grass from the base of the trees and he now maintains a well-fertilized and mulched area about one square metre/3×3ft grass- and weed-free. This is almost a necessity with this semi-dwarf stock. The weeding of these bare soil areas is kept to a minimum by holding the grass back with a patent timber edging, effectively a subterranean fence, which goes down lower than the grass roots but is almost invisible to the visitor.

The choice for replanting a short avenue in 1983 was a new local variety, 'Norfolk Royal Russet', which was discovered by a retired clergyman at Burnham Overy Staithe on the north Norfolk Coast. Interestingly this originated not as a seedling but as a 'sport', a non-standard branch on a 'Norfolk Royal' tree. The sported fruit has the crisp fragrance of the variety, but a more pleasing, dry, russeted skin.

Over the past few years, Mr Bullock has made his own 'whip-and-tongue' grafts on to M11, a fairly vigorous stock which gives the trees a good start on Felbrigg's rather poor, light soil. The problem of a walled garden in a dry region is providing adequate water for the young trees, and lacking the labour of times past, the gardeners are often hard pressed in this respect. However, although the young trees may grow more slowly and the orchard trees and wall fruit bear less, they are perfectly healthy, having adapted to the conditions which apply.

At BERRINGTON HALL in Herefordshire a newly planted orchard in the walled garden includes dessert and culinary apple varieties, many of them of historic importance. This orchard marks a happy association between the NCCPG (National Council for the Conservation of Plants and Gardens) and the National Trust. Mr Stan Baldock of the NCCPG, a keen gardener, has done most of the grafting himself: 'mostly whip-and-tongue, a few wedge grafts'. The first trees were planted in 1987 'on strong MM106 stocks to make robust half-standards so that the mature orchard will be a pleasant place to walk within, and so we can mow beneath them.' There are also plans to plant species of crocus in the grass, and a hundred corms of thirty species have been selected. Because crocuses flower early, the leaves will have

---

THE PRIORWOOD ORCHARD WALK: Apples through the Ages

Priorwood Gardens in Melrose, Roxburghshire, Scotland, has a most interesting orchard attached to its herb and flower garden. It contains several large old trees, planted long ago, before the orchard came into the care of The National Trust for Scotland, which has carried out additional planting to make a display of considerable variety and form. Visitors can walk or picnic in this orchard and get to know some of the pleasures of historic fruits.

There is 'James Grieve' trained as a stepover tree, a 'Blenheim Orange' made into a fan, and an 'Ardean Russet' in a 3.6m/12ft high cordon – all modern work which joins ranks with a superb old pear espalier and some plum and pear fans on a very high and beautiful fruit wall.

The leaflet which describes the planting plan of the apples in this orchard takes the form of 'An Orchard Walk' which takes the visitor through the centuries from the earliest times to the present day. It begins with the crab apple and a Scottish wild apple known as the Scrog.

Two varieties are associated with the Romans: the beautiful 'Pomme d'Api' with its contrasting red and pale yellow skin, and 'Court Pendu Plat', a small, red, richly-flavoured and very late-flowering apple, useful for areas subject to late frosts. Both of these are still available from specialist nurseries.

The 'Old Pearmain', a sweet mid-season apple, thought to be the Pearmain variety mentioned in a deed dated 1204, and the large, ribbed, sharp-tasting Costard which was recorded later in the thirteenth century were both popular old English apples. The name 'coster-monger' was given to the sellers of costard apples, this appellation later extended to include any kind of barrow boy. The 'Oslin' is an old Scots apple said to have originated as a pippin (a tree grown from a pip) in Arbroath. 'Ribston Pippin', a delicious, firm, slightly russetted apple, which originated in Knaresborough at the beginning of the eighteenth century, was one of the most famous and popular apples in Britain until the

arrival of its offspring, the 'Cox's Orange Pippin.'

Another once renowned culinary apple which has now passed out of currency is 'Golden Noble', introduced in 1820. 'Wyken Pippin', which was probably first planted at the turn of the eighteenth century, and 'Margil', introduced to England about fifty years afterwards, are both trees of moderate growth. Indeed 'Margil' in particular is a small tree, giving an apple of excellent flavour, and would do well in modern day gardens. 'Ashmead's Kernel', a sweet, greeny yellow apple, covered with russetting, is still valued in cultivation.

Modern contributions to apple breeding are represented by the aromatic 'Suntan', 'Golden Delicious' and the sweet early variety 'Discovery'. Scottish regional apples include 'Galloway Pippin', the culinary 'Tower of Glamis' and a famous local speciality, 'White Melrose', an old tree which may be a descendant of a tree planted by the monks of adjacent Melrose Abbey.

died back before grass mowing starts in earnest, when cutting will take place at three-weekly intervals, keeping the height to about 35-50mm/1.5-2in.

There are currently fifty apple varieties at Berrington, twenty-one of them old Herefordshire kinds, the others widely grown in the county. All except 'King's Acre Pippin' (raised in 1904) were introduced before 1900. Herefordshire

A real orchard scene: blossom time at Sissinghurst, with pheasant's eye narcissus and lady's smock flowering in the grass.

was the home of the famous apple-grower Thomas Andrew Knight and several of his apples – 'Downton Pippin', 'Wormsley Grange' and 'Stoke Edith Pippin' – have been located, and grafting material negotiated. There are also a few pears, propagated from old trees (still bearing their hundred-year-old labels) at Holme Lacy House nearby. Some of these are very rare: 'Beurré Bosc' (also known as 'Calebasse Bosc'), 'Marguerite Marrilat', a juicy golden-yellow variety known in 1841, 'Beurré Rance' a russetted pear which was raised in about 1762, 'Beurré Baltet' and 'Madame Preval' as well as 'Beurré Superfin' which is a fine old variety, rated as 'one of the best half-dozen' pears by nurseryman and fruit connoisseur Edward Bunyard. This property was also the home of the famous Holme Lacy pear – 'probably the largest pear that ever existed' according to Trust Adviser Mr Tony Lord. This pear tree covered three quarters of an acre and bore crops of five to seven tons.

A nasty setback occurred at Berrington in 1988 when rams in a neighbouring field managed to invade the orchard and damaged six of the newly planted trees. There was considerable anxiety about how they would grow during the next season, but at least, no damage was caused below the graft. By the end of 1989, it was evident that all the trees which were damaged had begun to make new growth, the freshly grafted trees making a particularly good recovery. In the autumn of 1989 a further group of trees was planted. The orchard at Berrington is likely to become not only an important local resource, but of national significance as The National Fruit Trials in Kent come continually under threat of closure or restriction. The uncertain future of the nation's fruit collection at the National Fruit Trials prompted the National Council for the Conservation of Plants and Gardens to begin a survey of fruit varieties held by small collectors and amateur gardeners. They are beginning with apple varieties introduced before 1900. People with old varieties in their garden or orchard are being asked to send such details as they are aware of to Mr Stan Baldock (see page 105). He is asking for the names, the number of trees, and their whereabouts, their approximate age and, if possible, a description of the fruit and its time of ripening.

Another excellent collection of apples is grown at ERDDIG, near Wrexham in Clwyd, where a new orchard has been planted using ancient varieties which were specially propagated for the purpose. These trees are trained into the pyramid form and underplanted with daffodils and narcissi given by the National Trust for Scotland from their garden at THREAVE, in Dumfries and Galloway.

At Threave itself there is a small collection of Scottish pears with names we hardly ever hear about south of the border: 'Seggieden', 'Hessle', 'Flower of Minorgan', 'Drummond', 'Maggie Duncan', 'Craigs', 'Grey Auchen' and 'Grey Benvie' grow on dwarfing stock in a grassy orchard to the north of Threave House. This is the location of the Threave School of Gardening, a horticultural training centre, which specializes in the type of gardening required in Trust gardens. There are twenty old pears, which were collected from orchards in the Dundee and Perth region by the Scottish Horticultural and Research Institute, before they were passed on to Threave.

Mr Bill Hean, principal of the Gardening School is more engaged with the ornamental side of the large and beautifully managed gardens, but he recognizes the importance of conserving the rare Scottish fruits, which may be used for breeding stock in the future. Of the pears, he recommended the variety known – somewhat uninvitingly – as 'Chalk', and he noted that the old varieties in the Threave apple collection (among them 'Tower of Glamis', 'East Lothian Pippin' and 'Cambusnethan Pippin') appear to be hardier and more resistant to canker, which is a problem in northerly areas with high rainfall. The kitchen garden at Threave has a good selection of fruit and vegetables of more recent origin trained in various ways on walls and in the open.

The nineteenth-century records of plantings made in the time of the sixth Duke of Devonshire were consulted in the partial replanting of the new orchard at HARDWICK HALL in Derbyshire. Here they have planted standard pears:

'Packham's Triumph', 'Marie Louise' and 'Pitmaston Duchess'. There are also wild pears (*Pyrus communis*), which has small hard pears but makes a very shapely beautiful tree, growing up to a stately 18m/60ft. Apples include 'Rev. W. Wilks', 'Norfolk Beefing' and 'Duke of Devonshire'. They also have 'Oullin's Golden Gage', a yellow gage which originated in France and arrived in England at the Rivers nursery about the middle of the last century.

To renovate a neglected tree, cut out all the dead and obviously diseased wood. Then cut out awkward and crossing branches, shorten very tall ones to a convenient side branch and thin old, crowded fruiting spurs.

ANATOMY OF AN APPLE TREE

(B) One-year-old shoots: long bendy shoots growing outwards from a main branch. These have growth buds only – don't prune unless you plan to cut back the older wood behind, in which case the young wood will all come away too.

(A) Branch leaders extend the growth of the main branches. The usual pruning method entails cutting strong new shoots back by about one-third, if it is weak, a half if it is reasonably strong, and two-thirds if it is very vigorous.

(C) Two-year-old shoots: stronger, less pliable wood from the previous season's growth, with plumper fruit buds on them. Prune weaker shoots back to 2 or 3 buds; prune less on stronger shoots, leaving more buds.

(D) Older shoots: 3-4 years old with fruit spurs which have grown from previous year's fruit buds. Only cut these out to correct the shape of the tree if the branch crosses with another or is diseased at some point.

Knowing how your trees grow will enable you to prune wisely and keep them both healthy and cropping with the minimum of intervention. The illustration shows an apple tree, the kind known as 'spur fruiting' because it bears fruit on small spurs which come off the main branches. If you have a 'tip bearer' which bears all or most of its fruit on the branch tips, as do 'Bramley Seedling', 'George Cave' 'Worcester Pearmain', the pruning system is slightly different. The principal idea is to keep a continuous cycle of older fruiting wood and newly grown wood and to balance the pruning for shape and for productivity.

The Head Gardener Mr Robin Allan enjoys the orchard. 'It's nice to see large mature trees, though some of them are laden with disease because you can't reach into the tops.' Despite it being an old orchard, he has noticed no signs of replant disease, although some of the trees have some canker and blight. The grass is kept to 40-50mm/1.5-2in and the area around the base of the trunks (where creeping buttercup is a problem) is sprayed with the herbicide Roundup which contains glyphosate as the active chemical.

Cornish varieties of apple have been replanted at GLEN-DURGAN in the upper walled garden, and at COTEHELE, which houses an extensive collection of local varieties. At NUNNINGTON HALL in North Yorkshire, they are building a collection of older varieties of apple known to have been grown in Ryedale since about 1850, some of them known only from here. The first plantings took place in 1984 and consist of 'Dog's Snout', 'Cockpit', 'Yorkshire Beauty' and 'Gooseberry'. At the same time new graftings were made of

'Burr Knot', 'Green Balsam' and the famous 'Golden Pippin' (known from John Parkinson's account of it in 1629). Since then the gardener has changed and the new gardener, Mr Richard Squires, intends to carry on the planting programme, regrafting three of the trees which did not survive and getting other supplies of stock for grafting.

Like his predecessor, he will be looking out for trees which have a northern connection and which are not well known elsewhere. He hopes to complete a list of old orchards in the region of Nunnington which he may be able to visit for grafting material. One variety he would very much like to find is 'Simkin's Pippin', which originated only a few miles from Nunnington.

At ACORN BANK in Cumbria, northern apples occupy the lower part of the walled garden. Only a few of the oldest trees survive, but there are several which were planted in the 1930s and there are plans to make some local graftings to replant gaps. Mr Chris Braithwaite, the Head Gardener, is making sure that any trees which have to come out because of age, damage or disease are 'replanted with standards of the same variety'. There is not much disease, a fact which Mr Braithwaite surmises may be partly owing to the fact there are many varieties and that having been planted over a long period, the trees vary in age.

There are pears, plums, medlars, mulberries and morello cherries as well as apples at Acorn Bank. Mr Braithwaite likes the open-grown morellos, 'lovely in flower and fruit, and naturally a nice shape' – the latter something barely recognized by those of us with smaller gardens who only know the morello as a wall-trained tree. Newly planted trees at Acorn Bank are kept bare at the base for two to three years, after which the grass is allowed to come up to the trunk. Mr Braithwaite planted native wood anemones and other meadow flowers both in the orchard and the wild garden.

Some of the Trust gardens have themselves a connection with the history of certain fruit varieties. The orchardist and nurseryman Edward Bunyard wrote a survey in 1920 in which he described the 'Blickling' pear of the famous Norfolk garden as a delicious fruit, 'greeny yellow with russet around the eye', but pointed out that it requires a warm wall and careful thinning. He reported that it was said to have been introduced from Belgium by a monastic order; certainly it received an Award of Merit from the RHS in 1907. CROFT CASTLE has an eponymous apple though this is not a name which figures in the National Fruit Trials' apple register. 'Osterley Pippin', a pretty red-green slightly russeted apple, said to be a hybrid offspring of the 'Ribston Pippin', was raised at OSTERLEY PARK in Middlesex by Ellis and first described in 1831.

Among the most important fruit conservation projects embarked upon by the National Trust are those concerned with cider apples and perry pears. The huge number of varieties which used to be grown when fine ciders and perrys were esteemed and regularly consumed have dwindled to a sad relic. Mr Tony Lord, Adviser to the National Trust, considers perry pears such as 'Barland', which grows at WESTBURY, to be 'among the most magnificent and long-lived of all flowering trees'. Interestingly, the cider and perry varieties are very local in their distribution: those in Devon are quite distinct from the Cornish ones. At COTEHELE in Cornwall, the collection of Tamar valley apples contains several which are local vintage varieties.

Damsons are a fruit which is often overlooked, though at HARDWICK HALL two varieties have been planted: 'Merryweather' and 'Farleigh's Damson'. 'Merryweather', which comes from Southwell in Nottinghamshire, the town famous for its 'Bramley's Seedling', is the damson most generally available in nurseries. The blue-black fruits are large; indeed, it is now thought that it is probably not a true damson. Many damsons are closely associated with a locality though not a great deal of research has been made into their origins except in so far as they are a commercial crop.

Some, like 'Farleigh's Damson' (found by James Crittenden of Farleigh in Kent) were wildlings which were observed by nurserymen and brought into cultivation. All around the Vale of Aylesbury, you find isolated damson trees of the

'Aylesbury Prune' in old hedges, and the 'Cheshire Prune' is well known in the Manchester area. Mrs Brittan at the APPRENTICE HOUSE GARDEN at Quarry Bank Mill, in Styal, Cheshire, identified three old trees in the derelict old garden. They were decrepit and overgrown, but Mrs Brittan cleared away the undergrowth and pruned them back, and they began to produce their small, dark, sourpuss fruits again. This damson is synonymous with the 'Shropshire Damson', also believed to be an English native variety, which was first recorded in 1676.

Damsons are useful trees, pretty in flower, hardy and self-fertile. They have been used as windbreaks, especially for plum orchards, and also grow well in hedges. Since they require little attention they make a good tree for the gardener who favours a policy of non-interference. A single tree on its own will produce fruit, and they are also useful pollinators of mid- and late-season plums.

There are, of course, many sweet plums of ancient lineage threatened with extinction, some of them in existence only in old orchards. Several are grown at WESTBURY as wall fruit: the 'Grosse Reine Claude' (the greengage which dates from the early sixteenth century), 'Orleans' and the 'French Prune d'Agen' (which are equally old) and 'Fotheringham' (pre-1665). 'Catalonia', which was recorded before 1545, makes a splendid fan-trained tree at Westbury and the 'White Magnum Bonum', another variety from the sixteenth century, fruits splendidly there.

At CANONS ASHBY in Northamptonshire, where they are also growing a number of interesting fruit trees, which include Victorian varieties of pear trained on the walls, and a working apple and pear orchard, they have a section of plums from the *Mary Rose*, the ship which sank in Henry VIII's time and was recently raised and restored. Red and white 'Magnum Bonum' plums were among the food found on the ancient ship and are featured at Canons Ashby.

An attractive design at West Green House where low box hedges, like green bowls, enclose apple trees. Note the elaborate trained screen which can just be glimpsed behind.

Vine covered arches, grown at Powis Castle with pools of variegated herbs in the beds beneath.

In its historic collections, the National Trust gardeners and advisers have sought not only varieties from the past but species of fruit which are not much known or grown nowadays. An example of one of the rarest of these is the wild service tree which is a beautiful tree with a glossy leaf slightly like an elongated Norway maple, which ends in elegant points. It grows into a tall tree, eventually over 25m/80ft, and is found sparsely in woodlands all over England and Wales. The tiny fruits, sometimes called chequerberries, are eaten bletted, after the first frosts have softened them. They are crunchy, almost gritty in texture, and have a sweet, spicy taste. In the past they were used as an extra ingredient in the making of ale or used on their own to make a fermented drink. There is still a pub at Smarden in Kent called the The Chequers with a wild service tree in the garden. Wild service, planted at WESTBURY, is doing very well and has begun producing fruit.

The top two pictures are of Chaenomeles *(or Japanese quince) grown for ornament, though the small fruits can be made into a jam. Bottom: The true quince,* Cydonia oblongata.

An even rarer fruit is that from the two forms of *Sorbus domestica*, not known as domestic service, but as sorb apple and whitty pear, reflecting the different forms of the two distinct cultivars, one like small apples, the other bite-sized pears. Like wild service berries, these fruits develop their flavour when they have softened either on the tree or in storage indoors. I find them absolutely delicious, but they are hardly eaten nowadays. Even people who have trees seem not to eat the fruit, although the Hegartys at Hope End near Ledbury have planted *Sorbus domestica* with a view to serving them in their hotel. Older editions of Bean's *Trees and Shrubs in the British Isles* reprint a letter from Mr Burrell, gardener to the Duchess of Albany in 1883, stating that 'we are sending food fruits of the pear-shaped service for dessert at the present time'. *Sorbus domestica* is tall and handsome with pinnate leaves like those of the mountain ash. The young one at Westbury is particularly shapely, but it has not begun to fruit.

Another fruit which needs to soften before it is eaten is the medlar, and this is beginning to regain popularity as a garden tree. The nutty, spicy fruits are the size of a large crab apple, but dark brown and with long 'claws' – the persistent calyx of the flower. Medlars are excellent with port after a Christmas meal. The medlar is a small tree, ideal as an open-grown tree or to ornament a hedge in gardens without a lot of space. The large leaves are very handsome, and in late spring it is covered with flowers which are like those of a single rose, creamy-white with an almost crepe-like texture.

Quince is another old-fashioned fruit which is again being planted. Like the medlar, it is quite small, although old trees can have a wide spread. The pear-like fruits ripen to yellow and need cooking as a cheese or jam before they are edible. They are strongly fragrant. A few slices of quince make a delicious additon to an apple pie. Quince and medlars are planted in a number of National Trust gardens and orchards and present few problems of cultivation, being largely disease-resistant and pest-free. The quince will only produce good crops of fruit if it has some sun, but the medlar seems to do reasonably well even in semi-shade. Neither medlar nor quince needs pruning except to remove crossing branches and dead wood.

Mulberries black and white are not native to the British Isles but have become part of its history, mostly because of the plan of James I to start a silkworm industry based on mulberries. The enterprise failed not, as commonly believed, because the wrong sort of mulberry was imported (silkworms will feed on black or white mulberries, though they prefer the white species which were grown under James I) but because the silkworms themselves seem not to thrive in our damp climate. Mulberries very quickly take on an appearance of extreme old age which has led many gardeners to believe they own trees from the time of King James. They are very long-lived and it is not unlikely that there are still a few trees from the early seventeenth century, possibly one of the shattered trees in Charlton Park in Blackheath. Both black and white mulberries are found in National Trust gardens, the oldest at CLEVEDON COURT, Avon, CLIVEDEN, Buckinghamshire and CHARLECOTE PARK, Warwickshire. Indeed, they are still being planted at MOSELEY OLD HALL, WIGHTWICK MANOR and WESTBURY. A fruit which has passed out of culinary use, mulberries are almost impossible to obtain commercially, so it was heartening to find the Head Gardener, Mr David Lee, who lives at Moseley Old Hall, extolling the virtues of 'mulberry and apple pie made of fruits from the garden'.

Orchards of the past were often reached through a nuttery or nut alley of hazel nuts of different kinds. The nuttery at SISSINGHURST is famous, and used to be visited for its display of polyanthus, though since the soil became 'polyanthus sick', these have been replaced. The nut alley at UPTON is being restored and at Moseley Old Hall the nut walk has four hazel and cobnut varieties in it. The cultivated cobnut is derived from the hazel (*Corylus avellana*), which grows over most of Europe, and has short husks with a protruding nut; the filbert is descended from *C. maxima*, a species native to the Balkans and south-eastern Europe, but widely grown in its cultivated form. The husk of the filbert is at least as long as

The nuttery at Sissinghurst was for a long time underplanted with primulas, but when soil-borne disease became a problem these were replaced with other unrelated plants.

A black walnut grown at The Courts.
This North American species is grown more for its
timber than for its fruit which is edible,
but not valued as highly as the common walnut.

the nut within, and sometimes considerably exceeds its length. There are several named varieties still in cultivation (though the half-million acres of nut cultivation at the turn of the century dwindled to under a hundred thousand acres by 1965). 'Cosford' and 'Nottingham Cob' are good cobnuts; 'White Filbert', 'Red Filbert', 'Purple-leaved Filbert' and 'Kentish Cob' are filberts which are still available.

At WIMPOLE HALL, near Royston in Hertfordshire, there is a most interesting collection of walnut species and cultivars. Some of these were grafted from trees at ST JOHN'S JERUSALEM in Kent, a property which suffered considerably in the storm of October 1987. Even more unusual is the fig orchard at

TRELISSICK where a dozen or so figs grow in a walled enclosure. In addition to the well-known 'Brown Turkey', probably the most commonly cultivated fig in Britain, there is 'White Marseilles', a pale, pear-shaped, early-season fig with sweet, rich, almost transparent flesh. 'White Ischia' ripens slightly later with a red tinge to its greeny-white colouring; it is reputedly delicious, though not hardy except in sheltered gardens in the very mildest places in Britain. 'Negro Largo', another mid-season fig grown at Trelissick, has associations with another garden, now in the care of the National Trust – CLIVEDEN in Buckinghamshire, where it was first introduced in 1866 from overseas, it is said from Dalmatia (Yugoslavia). Black, as its name suggests, it is grown also in France and Italy and is a vigorous and very fertile tree.

The figs at Trelissick thrive in the mild climate, sheltered conditions and rather poor soil, but a variety such as 'Brown Turkey' can be grown in more northerly gardens where it crops readily and reliably, if planted in a sunny, protected place. 'White Marseilles' and 'Brunswick' can also be grown outdoors. Figs grown in Britain will fruit without fertilization, which means that these rather large trees can be placed in a choice position as a single specimen. They usually produce better fruit if their roots are constricted by planting in a tank or a 'box' made from 600mm/2ft concrete slabs. Fan-training figs looks attractive and gives the fruits a good chance to ripen by allowing more sun to them and providing warmth from the wall. The fruit takes two years to become properly ripe: the pea-sized fruits on the summer's shoots, are carried through the winter to develop during the following spring and summer and ripen in late summer.

Perhaps, over the years, interest in old-fashioned fruits and nut varieties will revive to the extent that we shall have nuts, medlars, and sorb apples regularly at the table.

A serene view of the orchard at Hardwick at blossom time.
The wildflower sward is not mown until later, except for the areas
around the newly planted trees. This is kept closely
mown or bare, to reduce competition.

THE HERB GARDEN

Botanists today define a herb as any plant which does not have a woody stem. This definition fits better with that of the earliest English gardeners than with today's popular parlance which tends to restrict 'herbs' to plants used for culinary flavouring. We are thus reclaiming the wider definitions of the past when we make our modern herb gardens and include in them flowers and bulbs as well as the strictly culinary herbs.

In the great sixteenth-century herbals, which made an important contribution to the knowledge of plants in England, the writers included a range of herbs native to Northern Europe which did not form part of the classic Greek and Roman repertoire. The principal subject-matter in the old herbals was the medicinal properties of certain plants – the physic herbs. Herbs picked from the wild or grown in physic gardens were the basis of medical treatment until this century, so it was important to be able to identify, grow and use them capably and correctly.

One of the earliest English plant works, William Turner's *Names of Herbs* (1548), included many of the plants we now commonly recognize as herbs (such as marjoram, hyssop and borage), but he also included peas, juniper and medlars, referring to their medicinal and other virtues and relating them to the works of classical writers. Gerard's *Herbal* (1597) and Parkinson's *Paradisus* (1629) were self-evidently books in which the appreciation of the decorative effect and garden value of plants was quite as important as their practical uses. For example, Gerard reports of tulips that there is nothing set down by ancient writers on 'the Vertues of the Tulipa's, but they are esteemed especially for the beauty of their floures'.

A key figure in sixteenth-century herbal literature was Dodoens, whose fine *Herbal* was published in English in 1578 in a scrupulously researched translation by Henry Lyte of LYTES CARY in Somerset. Much of Gerard's *Herbal* may have been based on an unacknowledged use of Dr Priest's translation of Dodoens' later work – known as the *Pemptades* (1583) – but his own contribution was a strong sense of enjoyment in the beauty of plants in addition to their other attributes. Indeed, the amended 1633 edition of his *Herbal* – in which Thomas Johnson corrected a number of errors and added some interesting notes – is still one of the most pleasing and aptly phrased books on herbs.

Above: The herb garden at Gunby Hall in summer with its attractive mix of roses and herbs. Opposite: A golden autumn afternoon in the extensive herb garden at Hardwick Hall.

Present-day pharmacopoeias make interesting, if somewhat dry, reading, listing medicinal drugs with their preparation and usages. Many synthesized drugs are based on those originally derived from physic herbs. A branch of pharmacology known as pharmacognosy is specifically concerned with the investigation of drugs of plant and animal origin. Pharmacognocists working at the University of Dublin on a most interesting programme of experiments have compared the chemistry of herbs with a reputation as remedial plants against others randomly selected. In every case they found that there was a justification for the claims made. Some herbal remedies have been questioned or put into disrepute not because they were unsuccessful but because it was not known how they worked. The action of a commonly used drug such as aspirin, originally derived from the bark of willows (*Salix* spp.), has only recently been analysed and the complex responses of plants and animals to salicylic acid researched. Aspirin is now regarded as crucial in the treatment of certain kinds of stroke. North American Indians had no knowledge of the complex chemical chain involved in the conversion of food into essential fatty acids; yet they put evening primrose oil to many of the same uses that it has in its present-day clinical role. It should be remembered, too, that it was the widespread relief claimed by migraine sufferers who were taking feverfew that provoked the London Migraine Clinic to research and validate its use.

The handsome herb garden at ACORN BANK in Cumbria specializes in physic herbs. Equally attractive, but different in style, the famous herb garden at Hatfield Palace, with its brier hedge, chamomile paths and standard honeysuckles, is integrated into the larger scented garden.

Herb gardens are places of beauty as well as use, an idea almost lost when the concept of growing garden produce is narrowed to culinary utilitarianism. Conversely, the aesthetic qualities can be overvalued and the practical virtues overlooked. In fact, in present-day Britain, their decorative aspect is more valued than their use, and many splendid herbs grow untouched as if they were purely ornamental because we have not yet reincorporated them into our diet. Fresh herbs are so very much better-tasting than dried ones, which (even if they were reasonably fresh in the shop) may sit staling for months in pretty little glass jars in the kitchen before being used. A thyme or marjoram plant in the garden will provide fresh leaves from spring to early autumn – and some, such as rosemary and sage, are evergreen or semi-evergreen, so provide us with winter leaves too.

On an everyday level it is now becoming generally more accepted that diet is an important factor in general health. It would do us much good if we viewed our herb garden as a source of easily accessible snacks and flavourings. For a busy person a roll and butter with a few leaves of thyme, chives, marjoram, parsley or fennel makes a most enjoyable light lunch. All these herbs are scientifically accredited with beneficial effects on the digestive system. The link between the medical and the culinary is blurred.

It was common for country estates up to the eighteenth century to have a separate physic garden – the one at CALKE ABBEY (used as a kitchen garden since the last war) covered a substantial one-and-a-half acres. With changes in garden fashion and medical practice, many fell into a state of neglect. During this century, there has been a considerable movement towards the restoration and revival of herb gardens, which owes much of its success to the writings and practical example of Eleanour Sinclair Rohde in the 1920s and '30s. She drew attention to the many virtues of herbs in the garden, wrote about the herbalist tradition and designed many herb gardens. Thanks to the efforts of Miss Rohde and her followers, the pleasant and useful herb plants which were cultivated native plants, or introduced Mediterranean species, neglected in favour of more brightly coloured ornamentals, have come back into fashion.

Vita Sackville-West incorporated a herb garden into her plans for SISSINGHURST; 'a new herb garden with grass paths, clematis on trellis' occurs in her garden notebook. It took her from 1938 until 1947 to complete it and this was the first

The herb garden at Acorn Bank: a bright mixture of foliage and colour in high summer when herbs are at their best, the flowers overflowing over the pathways.

property with a working herb garden to be taken on by the National Trust. The paths of the herb garden are now paved (a necessity with the huge number of visitors) and the clematis plan was apparently never put into action, but the herb garden itself remains one of the most popular features of this much-visited garden.

In the 1960s the National Trust began to make its own collection of 'physic herbs' on the site of the enclosed vegetable garden at ACORN BANK, Temple Sowerby in Cumbria. In the days before the formation of the National Council for the Conservation of Plants and Gardens (NCCPG), to establish a representative collection of such medicinal and culinary herbs was pioneering work. It is still a significant collection – probably the most important in the north of England – but one which is not in use, unless one counts Mr Chris Braithwaite's application of wound herbs when he bruises or nicks himself while gardening. Many herbs have a reputation for staunching the flow of blood and aiding skin healing, but Mr Braithwaite mostly uses 'self-heal or lady's mantle – wrapping a leaf around the wound'.

As beautiful as any ornamental border, the collection is closely planted in three long south-west facing beds. A sunny sheltered bed against a wall provides good conditions for warm-climate herbs which originate from the Mediterranean, although Mr Braithwaite finds it quite demanding to achieve a succession of bloom in this bed. Damson trees, cherry laurel and guelder rose provide height, and tall herbs such as lovage, globe artichoke, mullein, angelica and teasels and climbers such as hops and honeysuckle add variety. There are richly bushy plants such as goat's-rue, Damask rose and deadly nightshade, and dainty flowerers such as musk mallow, chicory and sweet Cicely. Evergreen rosemary and juniper and bay give a range of darker greens, and greys and silver are provided by artemisias, *Eryngium* and the lavenders and sages. Thymes, lawn chamomile and small mints occupy the front of the beds with slightly taller plants such as marjoram and summer and winter savory. Mr Braithwaite experiments with the placing of the herbs, encouraging self-seeding and replanting elsewhere if a plant fails to thrive.

ACORN BANK: ANATOMY OF A HERB GARDEN
An early plan for part of the sunny south-facing bed.

1. Laburnum (*Laburnum × watereri 'Vossii'*)
2. Danewort (*Sambucus ebulus*)
3. Witch hazel (*Hamamelis virginiana*)
4. Summer savory (*Satureja hortensis*)
5. Hedge hyssop (*Gratiola officinalis*)
6. Sea holly (*Eryngium maritimum*)
7. Cranesbill root (*Geranium maculatum*)
8. White asphodel/bugbane (*Asphodelus cerasiferus*)
9. Elecampane (*Inula helenium*)
10. Basil thyme (*Acinos alpinus meridionalis*)
11. Sweet basil (*Ocimum basilicum*)
12. Chicory (*Cichorium intybus*)
13. Bay (*Laurus nobilis*)
14. Musk mallow (*Malva moschata*)
15. Clary sage (*Salvia horminum*)
16. Globe artichoke (*Cynara scolymus*)
17. Scotch chamomile (*Chamaemelum nobile*)
18. Goat's rue (*Galega officinalis*)
19. Mountain spinach (*Atriplex hortensis*)
20. English chamomile (*Chamaemelum nobile 'Plenum'*)
21. Golden variegated sage (*Salvia officinalis 'Icterina'*)
22. Redspur valerian (*Centranthus ruber*)
23. Angelica (*Angelica archangelica*)
24. Damask rose (*Rosa damascena trigintipetala*)
25. Hercules club (*Aralia spinosa*)
26. Sweet Cicely (*Myrrhis odorata*)
27. Lawn chamomile (*Chamaemelum nobile 'Treneague'*)
28. Bilberry (*Vaccinium myrtillus*)
29. Deadly nightshade (*Atropa belladonna*)
30. Thyme (*Thymus vulgaris*)
31. Cone flower (*Rudbeckia*)
32. Thorn apple (*Datura stramonium*)
33. French lavender (*Lavandula stoechas*)
34. Dogwood (*Cornus stolonifera*)
35. Evening primrose (*Oenothera biennis*)
36. Cotton lavender (*Santolina chamaecyparissus*)
37. Marjoram (*Origanum marjorana*)
38. Wild indigo (*Baptisia tinctoria*)
39. Great mullein (*Verbascum thapsus*)
40. Bitter candytuft (*Iberis amara*)
41. Virginian pokeweed (*Phytolacca decandra*)
42. Mezereon (*Daphne mezereum*)
43. Black root (*Leptandra virginica*)
44. Yellow loosestrife (*Lysimachia vulgaris*)
45. Juniper (*Juniperus communis*)
46. Golden Thyme (*Thymus vulgaris 'Aureus'*)
47. Horehound (*Marrubium vulgare*)
48. Teasel (*Dipsacus fullonum*)
49. Woad (*Isatis tinctoria*)
50. Madder (*Rubia tinctoria*)
51. Variegated balm (*Melissa officinalis 'Aurea'*)
52. Lovage (*Levisticum vulgare*)
53. Wood sanicle (*Sanicula europaea*)
54. Blue flax (*Linum perenne*)
55. Fennel (*Foeniculum vulgare*)
56. Southernwood (*Artemisia abrotanum*)

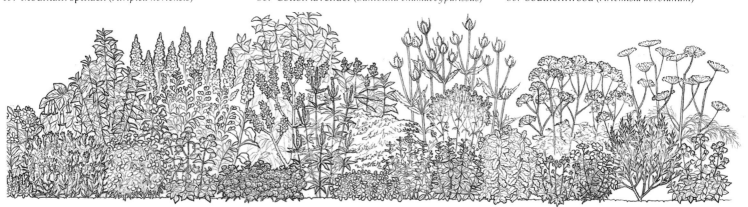

They have also had considerable success at Acorn Bank with some of the more unusual herbs. The rare *Veratrum album* thrives in the shady bed, its pleated leaves unfolding in the late spring, the sprays of white flowers making their contribution in late summer. A new project is the making of an 'American bed' assembling a collection of herbs from North America. There is pokeweed (*Phytolacca americana*), the robust purple agrimony (*Eupatorium purpureum* – called in its native parts gravelweed, since it is a remedy for urinary disorders ('gravels' was the term used for the stone-like concretions of minerals and salts which collect in the kidneys and bladder, with painful effect). Also part of the collection are horse-balm (*Collinsonia canadensis*) and the rudbeckia-like *Echinacea angustifolia*, the rhizomes of which were used in Indian medicine – and which are much loved by the Acorn Bank slugs. One of the rarest acquisitions is golden seal (*Hydrastis canadensis*), a plant of great herbal renown, now rare in the wild.

In severe weather, some of the plants, (notably the sages and some of the thymes) will be lost, but in recent mild winters, most things have come through and raced early into leaf. Since he came to Acorn Bank in 1982 Mr Braithwaite has learned to accept the Cumbrian weather, and to propagate plants not reliably hardy every autumn. Indeed, he has been so successful that the problem is not spring gappiness but rather that there is no longer any space left to plant new herbs in the garden.

Even when the herb garden is not an advertised feature within a garden, visitors show considerable interest. This has been the case at FELBRIGG, where the Assistant Gardener Mr Mark Neale, who has made herbs his particular subject has been encouraged by Mr Bullock to build up a herb collection within the walled garden. The dry soil and sheltered conditions suit the thymes, which include common, lemon, golden and orange sorts with mat-forming species such as *Thymus lanuginosus* and *T. serpyllum*.

Other Trust gardens have herb gardens which are designed to be principally ornamental, though they may have a

The old well-head makes a fine centrepiece for the herb beds in the courtyard of the medieval castle at Scotney. The beds were designed by Mrs Christopher Hussey and Lanning Roper.

theme. SCOTNEY CASTLE, in Kent, has a circular herb garden cut by grass paths designed by Mrs Christopher Hussey and Lanning Roper in 1970 around an old well-head in a sunny space sheltered by the walls of the 'ruined' castle. The herbs there have been chosen to include ones which would have been available at the time of the original fortified fourteenth-century castle at Scotney. Bulbs and annual plants add extra colour early and late in the year.

Smaller herb gardens often look better for having a fairly formal layout: a good example is the one at MOSELEY OLD HALL in Staffordshire. This is enclosed by box hedges within which are two beds measuring about 3.6×1.2m/12×4ft and a herbal parterre planted with thymes, camomiles and parsley (the feverfew was removed as it grew too large).

Although some of the great statuesque herbs such as angelica and lovage are too bulky for a small garden, one can choose carefully and include most of the important culinary herbs in a restricted space though it is necessary to make sure through a careful regime of pruning and dividing that the larger ones don't bully their smaller neighbours. Even if one discounts their usefulness in the kitchen, herbs are very good at filling awkward spaces and indeed can be grown to great advantage in small and narrow beds, perhaps bordering a path where their spread is contained, and they are easily accessible if you wish to gather or pick them. Mints, cotton lavender and southernwood make a wonderfully bushy display and if they start to threaten the path, you can simply take the shears to them. It is a good idea, in any case, once you are past mid-summer and the bushy herbs are looking blowzy, to reduce them to a neat compactness from which new growth springs. This will look fresh until the frosts come.

It is worth experimenting with herbs. Town gardens are often quite shaded, leading their owners to believe that it is impossible for them to grow herbs. Contrary to expectation, this is often untrue, for although many herbs originate in dry sunny places, they can be remarkably tolerant. Mint, southernwood and rue will certainly grow in semi-shade and can,

with careful pruning to prevent legginess, even be coaxed to do quite well in fairly deep shade. In fact, Mr Braithwaite believes his shady herb beds at Acorn Bank to be rather better than his drier wall-sheltered places for herb-growing.

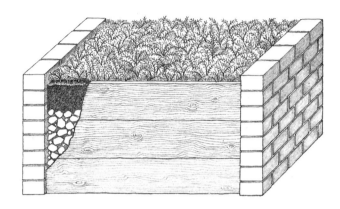

A herb bench can be situated out in the open, or preferably against a sheltered, sunny wall. Filled to within about a brick's height with rubble to ensure good drainage, it is topped up with compost or loam. The kind of chamomile called 'Treneague' (low-growing and apple-scented) is the best to use for planting but it needs to be carefully weeded and bedded down with extra compost at the end of the autumn.

A herb hanging basket is surprisingly effective for its visual appeal and practical use. Several kinds of herb may be used, for example, bright green parsley, a small grey-leaved sage, marjoram and thyme.

*A close-up view inside Hardwick Hall herb
garden showing the tower-like shapes of hops grown over tall
quadripods casting long shadows over the other plants.*

At HARDWICK HALL, a nationally famous herb garden is integrated with a potager-style selection of vegetable and ornamental plants. It is large, since the original gardens were extended and elaborated during the mid-1970s. About half the plants in it are those which would have been present in an Elizabethan garden such as Bess of Hardwick would have known. The herbs (mainly culinary) are grown in a fairly formal arrangement in the two-section garden area, each symmetrically balanced with a square central bed surrounded by herb borders, high points created by naturally tall herbs such as fennel, elecampane and bay or by tripods draped with hops.

It is now, after fifteen years or so, that some disadvantages to this beautifully conceived but somewhat static system are being perceived. The Head Gardener Mr Robin Allan has noticed that plants in the labiate family (hyssop, sages, lavenders and mints) appear to be suffering from a kind of replant disease. The young plants grow vigorously for a while and then collapse. Mr Allan points out that 'some plants are naturally on the move'. Mints, for instance, 'tend to develop outwards at the edges of a clump, leaving a hollow centre' – nature's way of finding fresh soil. His solution until now has been to divide up large plants and to replant using quantities of leafmould, 'which seems to help', but he is also experimenting by replacing all the soil in the area earmarked for labiates. Herbs on the whole are fairly resistant to pests and diseases, but the sages have been recently plagued by leaf-hoppers, not usually present in large enough numbers to be a problem, but at Hardwick they have been taking the vigour out of the young plants. Perhaps more worrying is the emergence of red spider mite which proliferated even during the wet summer season of 1988 and – contrary to usual practice – transferred itself from plants out of doors (mainly primulas) to those inside.

These are problems which would be noticed by the gardener rather than the everyday visitor, who still finds Hardwick a delightful place to see these herbs, which include well over a hundred species and varieties. Annuals such as

Flowers and herbs in the walled garden at Buckland Abbey. This herb garden with its high sheltering walls dates back to the fifteenth century.

*A corner of Buckland Abbey herb garden showing the paths and formal box-edged
beds with their ornamental divisions and shapes, and the buttressed wall which creates sheltered alcoves.*

borage, poppies and pot marigolds are allowed to self-seed, plants being moved or thinned later. Others such as basil, marjoram, coriander and *Nicotiana* are raised under glass and planted out as well-grown seedlings in late spring. A number of herbs (hops, chives, comfrey, vervain, tansy, woodruff and valerian fall into this category) get too clumpy after a few years, so are divided and replanted, or grown again from seed, usually every three to five years depending on growth. Propagation by cuttings suits other herbs, such as mints (usually at about two- to three-year intervals), hyssop, common thyme and lemon thyme, the sages and santolinas (once every three to five years).

The gardeners cut some of the plants back in late summer to prolong the growth and tidy them up. Some such as angelica and tansy will flower again, and mint and alchemilla will make good new shoots under this treatment. This practice also has the effect of stopping the more rampageous plants from self-seeding. Angelica is not allowed to go to seed and they know the wisdom of keeping fennel cut back.

(A gardener in a Hampshire herb garden told me how he moved a fennel plant from one side of the garden to the other during late summer when it was beginning to set seed. The next year saw a trail of tiny fennel plants leading from the old to the new site, along the trail of the barrow.)

There are many styles of herb garden, which can be adapted to large and small areas, but there are no hard and fast rules unless that it is always to keep some herbs within easy march of the kitchen for gathering in unpleasant weather. At Springhill, in County Londonderry in Northern Ireland the walled herb garden is the nearest part of the gardens to the house. Herbs are generally speaking easy to grow and look attractive almost anywhere. Miss Sackville-West's remarks on dill can be applied to many other herbs:

'The correct place for dill is in the herb garden, but if you have not got a herb garden, it will take a very decorative place in any border. I like muddling things up: and if a herb looks nice in a border, then why not grow it there.'

A sprig of basil: a valuable herb which can be planted out in the open in spring, or raised in pots, especially in areas habituated by slugs who seem to relish it. The sweet basil, Ocimum basilicum *(above) is the kind most commonly grown, but purple basil tastes just as nice and the frilled kind known as 'Purple Ruffles' makes an attractive robust pot plant. Bush basil,* Ocimum minimum, *has small, fine leaves and has a longer season, and there is also a lemon scented species.*

THE POTAGER

During the last decade there has been more interest in vegetable gardens for their own sake and more experimentation with kinds of fruit and vegetables than for about a century. A good deal of attention has also been given to finding a style for the productive garden. It is only now that people have begun to realize that the cultivation of everyday garden produce can be done in a way which is aesthetically pleasing as well as productive.

Introducing the alien notion that a fruit and vegetable garden can be fun and pretty, as well as enjoyable to look at and to work in, Mrs Rosemary Verey's potager at Barnsley House near Bibury in Gloucestershire has been one of the most influential vegetable gardens of the decade. However, once the idea was in currency, its appeal was widespread and many visitors to the attractive and fertile potager at Barnsley went home to adapt and restyle their own gardens in a similar fashion.

At the same time vegetables and modes of growing new to England were being researched by the horticulturalist and writer Miss Joy Larkcom from her experimental market garden in Suffolk. She has grown and introduced to a larger public many salad greens and vegetables from China and Japan. She has in addition experimented widely with the potager form on a small scale using perennials, summer and winter greens and roots.

A third strand to this new style of cultivating produce has been interest in dense cropping on narrow beds which are

Making an ornament of utility: a lovely octagonal fruit cage at West Green House. The old-fashioned lantern cloches are similarly not only elegant but functional, and are, in fact, more adaptable than the modern cloche.

carefully tended and fertilized. The most confusing aspect of this development is its nomenclature, for it has been variously known as raised beds, deep beds and the intensive bed system. It now seems to have settled as the deep beds system. Used both by the Chinese, who knew how to maximize space, and by the French urban gardeners in the nineteenth century, the system simply involves keeping small areas fertile and productive by adding compost. The beds are laid out with small paths leading around them from which any part of the bed may be reached without ever treading on the soil and compacting it. Close planting in this rich soil gives good crops and dense leaf cover which inhibits weeds. The dimensions are generally about 1.5m/5ft (or less depending on a comfortable working stretch for one's arms) by say 3-3.5m/10 or 12ft. This method lends itself to use in an ornamental potager since the beds do not necessarily need to be rectangular, but can be adapted to whatever decorative design is required.

Compost applied regularly to these deep beds to keep a high level of fertility has the effect of giving them a profile above that of the paths around them. The soil can be further raised and held in place by building a wooden frame around the bed. When this is done the final effect looks very similar to the 'raised beds' of medieval times which we see in old manuscripts, Books of Hours and gardening books of the seventeenth century. From what we can gather from pictures and documentary evidence, the medieval raised beds were 'sparse planted', especially as regards ornamental flowers; each plant allocated ample space, so that its full shape and form could be appreciated. At Stafford Castle a medieval garden is being recreated with precise regard for historical

*A milky-green spaghetti marrow ripening
at Barrington Court among the five-fingered foliage and
golden tufts of tropaeolum.*

Chelsea Show exemplified different ways of developing the theme. As early as 1984, Mrs Rosemary Verey designed a tempting fruit garden for the Gloucestershire fruit specialists, Highfield Nurseries, which had a range of interestingly shaped trees with apple alleys with lettuces and herbs nestling at their bases. In 1988 Ms Jacqui Moon and Mr John Ravenscroft's popular overall award winner at the 75th show was a nostalgically planted cottage garden with flowers, fruits and vegetables, in a pleasantly assorted mixture. There were herbs, lupins, beans and roses, a beehive, red currants, columbines and rhubarb and two large terracotta forcing pots.

Part of the inspiration for such a garden is the old cottage garden as depicted in the paintings of Helen Allingham at the turn of the century, romantic in their theme (even in the late eighteenth century, the rural idyll was a nostalgic subject) but precise in the plants, many of which can be identified from the painting. The ideal for the cottage garden was a happy mixture of flowers, fruit and vegetables, though flowers tended to predominate almost exclusively in many of the paintings, and the family pig, an important part of the rural economy, was rarely painted, though chickens and ducks were considered acceptable. Flora Thompson in *Lark Rise to Candleford* gives a description of apple and pear trees, currants, raspberries and gooseberries, and rows of broad beans, cabbage, parsley, rosemary and chives, growing adjacent to flowers such as lilies, phlox, wallflowers and Michaelmas daises, pansies, hollyhocks and lily of the valley.

The other strand of inspiration is formal and French, drawing in particular, from the great gardens at Versailles and Villandry. The Potager du Roi at Versailles has been conserved to the original late-seventeenth-century design of la Quintinie, gardener to Louis XIV. In addition to creating this famous potager on a grand scale with separate enclosures for different kinds of fruits and vegetables, la

accuracy. There are sixteen rectangular raised beds in it as well as an arbour, mount, chamomile seat and flower meadow, with an orchard of costard apples and Warden pears adjoining. At Hatfield, in part of her private garden, the Marchioness of Salisbury has also established a series of raised beds, where herbs and vegetables are grown, surrounded by espaliered fruit.

The combination of new practical ideas, advances in plant and soil science and imaginative design has brought us into one of the most exciting periods of fruit and vegetable growing. Two award-winning model garden exhibits at the

*Marrows will climb as well as sprawl, and growing them
vertically to make an attractive screen or tunnel is a good plan in
a smaller garden. Here, the climbing companion to the vegetable
spaghetti at Barrington Court is nasturtium.*

A view of the elaborate potager at Villandry, showing the red rose standards and beds of green 'Cos' lettuce and red 'Salad Bowl' in the foreground. The pear trees are trained into an elongated oval shape on a short leg of trunk which they call 'en quenouilles'.

Quintinie wrote an important book on fruit and vegetable gardens which was translated into English by John Evelyn as *The Compleat Gardener*. At Villandry the famous potager extends along the south bank of the Loire, near Tours. The Carvallo family have created an intricate Renaissance-style vegetable garden conceived by Dr Joachim Carvallo when he purchased the château and estate in 1906. Built on a grand scale, this garden of 15,000 square yards is divided into nine equal squares separated by wide alleys with large bowers and fountains at the internal intersections. There is another fountain at the centre of each of the square compartments (now dry, but used in the past as a fount for watering the plants). The compartments are bounded by low stepover espaliers and subdivided internally into geometric shapes edged with dwarf box, with narrow pathways in between. Inside these intricate divisions the vegetables make patterns of colour and shape as glorious and desirable as those in any border.

Flowers such as verbena, petunia and polyanthus are used in blocks and make a contrast with the vegetables, but mostly it is the vegetable foliage itself which creates the effect. There are blue-greens of broad beans, kales and cabbage, and lettuce in bright greens and reds ('Salad Bowl' and 'Lollo' and 'Cos'). Green peppers, white and red chard, glossy strawberries and golden celery all make their effect and textures are played off against each other – the crisp cabbage shapes, the linear onions, feathery carrots. Each year, a plan of the garden is made, an artful mosaic which takes in crop rotation as well as a balance of colour and form in its composition.

This elaborate arrangement is given height by the pear trees which are trained like a bushy upright cordon, to about the height of a person, and by standard rose trees. In winter the beds are cleared but the structure is so good and the

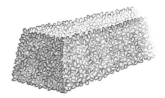

The box used in the low hedges of the potager at Villandry and in many National Trust gardens is not common box but a dwarf variety called 'Suffruticosa' which makes a neater small hedge. Expensive to buy, it can be raised quite easily from cuttings, and a hedge can be made in a few years from a few 'parent' bushes.

distinct shapes of the denuded trees, the box-edged beds and arbours are such that it still looks attractive, especially with the frost and snow bringing out the pure outlines of the beds and paths.

This beautiful potager with its elegant château and other gardens is maintained by means of admission fees, so visitors are encouraged. In fact, there are now only seven gardeners, who trim the vines and box and are responsible for all the vegetables. They do all the weeding by hand and use no chemicals, believing them to be incompatible with healthy box hedges. Some of the produce grown in the garden is consumed by the family themselves and by their domestic staff and the gardeners and their families. The large surplus is made up into large compost heaps along with cow manure from the adjacent farm. This compost, applied in spring, ensures high soil fertility.

This elegant masterpiece at Villandry was the inspiration for Mrs Rosemary Verey, but her potager at Barnsley House is very much her own personal style. Her paths are of brick, laid in patterns of different colours and textures. The beds themselves are on a much smaller scale, many of them edged with dwarf box, others decorated with ornamental cabbage. Goblet apple trees and roses give height within the garden, which has two trellised arbours, covered with golden hop and the ornamental vine *Vitis coignetiae*. Herbs, the decorative oak-leaved 'Salad Bowl' lettuce in red and green forms, the silver and red chard, as well as broad and runner

Cottagers' Kale from the Apprentice House Garden at Styal. A very hardy, old variety, it is now being grown for foliage beauty as well as use.

beans and courgettes, each play their role within a smaller, more intricate design.

Miss Joy Larkcom's several potagers in Suffolk are smaller affairs arranged more on a cottage-garden method of patterning, although she allows good plants to self-seed and the whole effect is of a strong design, slightly disarrayed. Her summer potager is on a very much smaller scale than Mrs Verey's, though it includes the same elements – arches and narrow paths, and small beds subdivided into smaller shapes. She calls it her 'petit potager', a successful experiment to see if the idea of an ornamental vegetable garden could be carried out on as small a scale as would be allowed within the garden of an average modern house. In winter as the frosts begin to bite, the flowers and summer vegetables die back exposing the lines and curves of paths and arches, broken here and there by an evergreen such as rosemary.

A short distance away, the winter garden contains among other things, chicories, endives, *Montia perfoliata*, leeks and winter savory. One of the last plants to die back, and the most forward in spring, is tangy buckler-leaved sorrel. The plants grow in an arrangement of neat rectangular beds, like those in medieval pictures. Miss Larkcom has found spun polypropylene fleece to be very effective in protecting her winter crops from damage from the harsh East Anglian winds, which otherwise makes them rather dirty and dog-eared. With this minor accessory she finds she can pick salads from these gardens all year round, experimenting with new plants such as 'Mibuna' (which has long leaves, spicy and slightly nutty-tasting), a long-rooted radish called 'Beauty Heart' (pale greeny white with a purple-starred centre), and 'Tendergreen' (a good winter plant which is harvested leaf by leaf), many different sorts of Chinese cabbages and purple Brussels sprouts.

Many of the plants grown in potagers are crops which can be harvested a few leaves at a time, with the plant *in situ* – 'Salad Bowl' lettuce and French sorrel are examples. By this means the potager can be used without destroying its patterning. Cut-and-come-again lettuces and chicories which are severed low on the stem and left to resprout can be cropped in pairs to preserve symmetry. With other vegetables such as leeks and carrots, alternate plants can be taken up from a row, or a small block can be removed at a time.

There were strange purple bean-like climbers growing up a tripod at TINTINHULL HOUSE in Somerset when I visited the kitchen garden there. Seeing them from a distance I thought they were a variety of runner bean, but they proved to be *Dolichos lablab* – used ornamentally here, but developed as a fodder plant in its native Africa. Tintinhull is a compromise between a potager and an English kitchen garden, with plain vegetable areas surrounded by groups and borders of flowering plants and shrubs. There are rows of potatoes,

Leeks at the Apprentice House Garden at Styal, inter-cropped with cabbage. When the leeks have been pulled, the young cabbages will fill the space as they grow to maturity.

The kitchen garden at Tintinhull. Neat rows of carrot, onions and other vegetables grow alongside irises bedded in rows before being planted in the main ornamental garden. Large herbs and ornamentals, such as euphorbia, grow on the margins of the vegetable plot and a bright edging is made from catmint.

beetroot, carrots, leeks, cauliflowers and lettuces, but the plot is edged in a purple mist of *Nepeta* 'Six Hills Giant' and there are roses where the paths cross. Irises are lined out next to the broccoli and peonies next to the sprouts.

The gardener and writer Mrs Penelope Hobhouse and her husband Professor John Malins (the National Trust tenants at this property) are strict about self-seeding flowers among the vegetables: they believe a vegetable bed should be 'neat and completely weed-free'. The restrained, tidy rows of vegetables contrast strikingly with the unruly and informal flowers which make an edging and a backdrop for them. There are small surprising events among the flowers, such as a copper urn with an elegant *Campanula pyramidalis* rising from it, and a patch of the grass *Ophiopogon planiscapus nigrescens* with its purple-black leaves. There are violas and the small *Geranium striatum* dotted here and there among the dark leaves of hellebore and peony, and smaller, paler clumps of Jacob's ladder with its pinnate leaves and blue flowers. The pretty, dark, purple heads of *Verbena bonariensis* dot the edgings of flowers: this verbena is a perennial, but not reliably hardy except in very sheltered warm areas; in Somerset it self-seeds in mild winters, but usually has to be raised afresh each year. Sweet peas are grown – like the *Dolichos lablab* – up tripods, which are placed symmetrically round the vegetable plots. Lilies and irises add their touch of glamour, and later in the season Japanese anemones lighten the garden with their luminous blooms.

The larger herbs are given their head, so there are shapely bushes of rosemary and tall angelica. Fruit in the kitchen garden is confined to autumn-fruiting raspberries for their welcome late-season crop, and pears trained as espaliers which serve to make an ornamental divide between parts of the garden. To the south of the kitchen garden, a gate leads to an orchard. Fruit trees are interplanted with rare ornamental trees, planted by Professor Malins. Sheep graze peacefully

The rhubarb garden at Barrington Court
has handsome terra-cotta forcing jars in place over the plants.

A few sticks of forced rhubarb. The crop can be
ready to eat as early as January in a mild year, but the forcing jars
should be used only every 2-3 years on the same plant.

here, contributing to an idyllic scene (but making strong guards on young trees a necessity).

Another garden which has a strong tradition of growing flowers, intermingled with fruits and vegetables in imaginative combinations, is that at KELLIE CASTLE in Fife, which belongs to The National Trust for Scotland. This is a late Victorian garden which has been restored with many of its original features and planting designs. The kitchen produce is grown not in a single area but in separate beds in various parts of the garden surrounded by lawns, flower borders and roses. Among the vegetables they raise are three kinds of potato, parsnips, carrots, cauliflower, cabbages, leeks, onions, spinach and lettuce. Globe artichokes are also grown, their handsome silver-grey foliage no trial for any gardener to accommodate, whether in flower border or potager.

Flowers and fruit are often grown in association: 'clematis, roses and honeysuckle growing up apple, plum and damson trees'. Thirteen varieties of apple are to be found in the garden and several plums and pears. There are wall red currants and gooseberries grown as wall fruit, a mode of growing not much practised nowadays, but very ornamental. At Kellie these bushes are usually underplanted with pinks and primulas. However, when doing the planting, care must be taken to disturb the soil as little as possible; it must also be kept fertile, for currants and gooseberries are shallow-rooted and hungry plants. A combination which has recently been tried out is a planting of tayberries alongside the climbing roses which cover the rose arches. The result of this anti-apartheid policy, according to the head gardener Mr Alan Cumming, is 'a gay intermingling of flowers and coloured foliage which has proved very effective, though not easy to plan'.

There are a few other Trust gardens which draw visitors to their fruit and vegetable displays. BARRINGTON COURT devotes considerable attention to its productive garden. One can see sea kale and rhubarbs and herbs at GUNBY HALL in Lincolnshire, and old apple and pear trees in the old orchard and walled garden. WEST GREEN HOUSE in Hampshire also has old fruit trees, mostly apples, and in this attractive walled garden may be seen a remarkable, elegantly ornamental fruit cage. West Green has developed a beautiful English potager style which mixes flowers, herbs and fruits – including standard gooseberries.

A standard gooseberry, with its bushy head on a long stem, looks like a kind of green lollipop hung in season with the plump round globes of ripe dessert gooseberries. It is possible to buy a gooseberry already pruned as for a cordon (single stem) from a good nursery, but most come in bush

form which means that you will need to select a strong central shoot which will be the main stem and carefully slice off the other stems. Most standard gooseberries are grown on a rootstock of other *Ribes* (*R. aureum* or *R. divaricatum*) but it is possible to make them from plants grown on their own roots – even from your own cuttings.

A STANDARD GOOSEBERRY

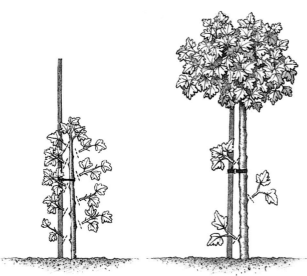

(A) Plant your gooseberry in late autumn/winter, in a pot or in the ground. Tie the single shoot to a stout cane. During the summer, remove the side shoots and tie in the lengthening stem. The plant will require the support of the stake throughout its life, so choose a handsome one or you will spoil its attractiveness.

(B) Continue to remove lower side shoots and when the stem reaches the desired height (usually 1-1.2m/3-4ft) pinch out the growing tip, which will have the effect of causing the top to bush out. The round, bushy top is kept in trim by pruning all the shoots to 5 leaves in late June. Thinning shoots overall can also be carried out to let more air and light in. However, retaining bushiness tends to deter birds from picking the fruits.

Trained pears flank the colourful border at Barrington Court, making a useful back screen. Open-grown fruit makes a good screen but requires a very stout post and wiring system to support it.

THE KITCHEN GARDEN

Grand houses in the past, occupied by large families and parties of house guests, required large kitchen gardens to serve them. It is interesting to look at illustrations of country houses and see how at first the kitchen garden and orchards were perceived as beautiful, pleasureable places and situated close to the houses, and then as the landscape movement came in during the eighteenth century, they were set behind walls, and moved to a position well out of sight. The large old kitchen garden at CALKE ABBEY even had a tunnel for the use of the staff so that the comings and goings to the garden went unseen by anyone in the house or pleasure garden.

Such large gardens produced quantities of vegetables, herbs and fruit for the grand house and necessarily entailed large numbers of staff. Records still exist in many houses now under the management of the National Trust. At CLUMBER in Nottinghamshire twenty-eight gardeners were employed to run the kitchen garden alone. Horticultural staff are still not highly paid, but were the same number of staff to be employed in the present day the wage bill would cost the National Trust in the region of a quarter of a million pounds per annum.

Coats must be cut according to the cloth, and it has usually been the case that the kitchen gardens, perceived as 'too labour intensive' are the first to be run down. Much as one might regret their transformation into car parks, there is no doubt that a large area screened from view is an ideal place to locate cars in such a way as not to interfere with an historic

The simple rhythm of form and foliage
associated with the kitchen garden, represented by the splendid
rows of the cabbage crop at Barrington Court.

landscape. There are other considerations affecting kitchen garden closures: often the families who used to live in the houses are no longer there, or if they are, they rarely require the scale and style of the past produce.

There is also the undercurrent which has hung over from the landscape period, that fruit and vegetable gardening is really not quite nice, that raising rhododendrons or alpines was more meritorious and more the kind of thing visitors wanted to see. There are signs that this is changing, and that the revival of interest in kitchen gardens for their own sake is having its effect. Luckily the National Trust still has a few notable kitchen gardens which are being run with new interest and imagination.

One of the most exciting of these is at UPTON HOUSE in Warwickshire, where the terrace overlooks a marvellous high lawn which takes up the whole of the south front, cedars planted down banks to the side peep up over the grass, and the view southwards looks over wooded pasture. A beautiful country landscape, you think admiringly, but where on earth are the gardens? It is when the far end of the lawn is reached that the great dramatic surprise is sprung and a steep terrace yawning downward is revealed, decorated with dry banks planted with flowers and shrubs, dipping down to a pool enlarged from a medieval stew pond. At the heart of this area, making a magnificent centrepiece, is a huge vegetable garden sloping down towards the south.

It is thought that fruit and vegetables have been grown here since the original Tudor house was completed in 1695, which gives it a continuous history of cultivation of three hundred years. Until recently this kitchen garden produced

food for the family of Lord Bearsted, who left the house in 1987. A photograph dated 1904 shows it in very similar condition to the way it is today, its charming scheme a true English vegetable garden with its sloping rows of produce: its fruit blocks and lines of trees, gooseberry and currant bushes and lined-out cabbages, kale and onions. There is plenty of glass for cloches to protect early vegetables and glasshouses to raise young stocks so the garden always has something of interest to show.

Above: Artichokes flowering like this look attractive but are past eating. It is the young, blanched stems and the flower buds with the small tender 'choke' at their base which are eaten.

Opposite: A wide view of the beautiful kitchen garden at Upton House, an excellent example of a traditional productive garden with old and new style tree fruit, soft fruit, vegetables and herbs.

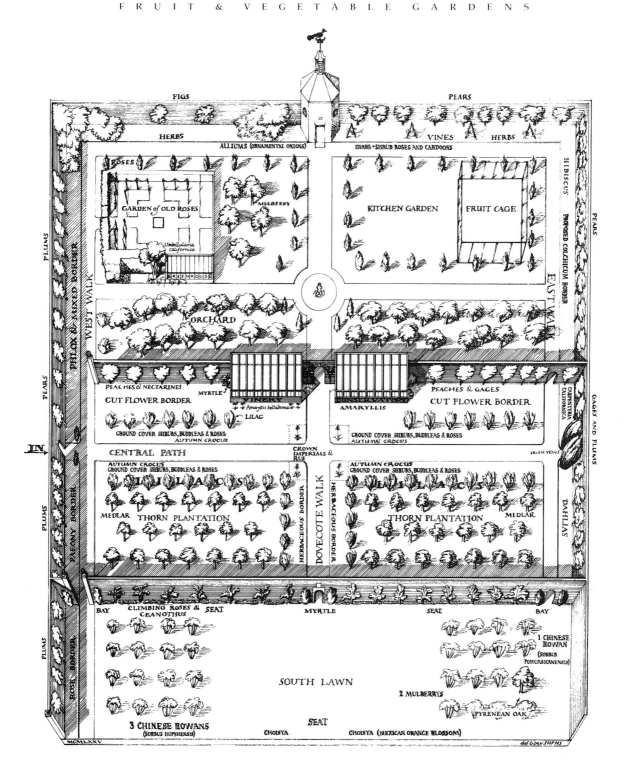

FIGS · PEARS

HERBS · VINES · HERBS

ALLIUMS (ORNAMENTAL ONIONS) · HERBS + SHRUB ROSES AND CARDOONS

ROSES

GARDEN of OLD ROSES

MULBERRY

KITCHEN GARDEN · FRUIT CAGE

Umbellularia californica

GREENHOUSE

HIBISCUS

PROPOSED COLCHICUM BORDER

PEARS

WEST WALK

PHLOX & MIXED BORDER

PLUMS

ORCHARD

EAST WALK

PEACHES & NECTARINES

CUT FLOWER BORDER

MYRTLE

VINERY

Amaryllis belladonna

LILAC

CONSERVATORY

AMARYLLIS

PEACHES & GAGES

CUT FLOWER BORDER

CARPENTERIA CALIFORNICA

GAGES AND PLUMS

GROUND COVER SHRUBS, BUDDLEAS & ROSES
AUTUMN CROCUS

GROUND COVER SHRUBS, BUDDLEAS & ROSES
AUTUMN CROCUS

PEARS

CENTRAL PATH

CROWN IMPERIALS & RUE

IRISH YEWS

IN

AUTUMN CROCUS
GROUND COVER SHRUBS, BUDDLEAS & ROSES

AUTUMN CROCUS
GROUND COVER SHRUBS, BUDDLEAS & ROSES

LILACS

LILACS

PLUMS

MEDLAR · THORN PLANTATION

HERBACEOUS BORDER

DOVECOTE WALK

HERBACEOUS BORDER

THORN PLANTATION · MEDLAR

DAHLIAS

PEONY BORDER

BAY · CLIMBING ROSES & CEANOTHUS · SEAT

MYRTLE

SEAT · BAY

ROSE BORDER

PLUMS

1 CHINESE ROWAN
(SORBUS POHUASHANENSIS)

SOUTH LAWN

2 MULBERRYS

PYRENEAN OAK

SEAT

3 CHINESE ROWANS
(SORBUS HUPEHENSIS)

CHOISYA · CHOISYA (MEXICAN ORANGE BLOSSOM)

MCMLXXV

del & inv JHFHS

Miss Sarah Cook, the young Head Gardener, has just recently taken over the management of Upton House garden. Among her staff she has two able helpers in Mr Alan Philpott and his father who have gardened all their working lives at Upton. The garden is divided in two by an east-west path, but the even line of the slopes is broken at intervals by large old apple trees. The whole area is open because they don't use fruit cages. 'The birds aren't bad,' notes Miss Cook; 'we don't have trouble with the raspberries, but we do always cover the strawberries with netting.' The gooseberry bushes are kept dense and bushy (not pruned and opened up) and this seems to deter bird predation adequately while producing plenty of fruit. They have grown 'Careless', 'Leveller' and 'Whinham's White' over a long period, propagating every few years on a rotation from existing stock. Even the currants, red, white and black, did well without a cage.

Soft fruit such as blackberry and loganberry is decoratively trained up the fruit wall of the old cherry garden, alongside plums and ornamental plants. Old apple trees are dotted over the vegetable garden. More recent trees such as 'Emneth Early', 'James Grieve' and 'Cox's Orange Pippin' are planted on dwarfing stock in a double row in the kitchen garden.

Why the onions do so much better on the capacious lower beds, the gardeners have so far found 'inexplicable', but since they do, it was decided 'the best practice was to move them about only within the lower area'. Runner beans are also planted down here but since they suffer from slug attacks, they are not planted out until they are in good leaf, and they are barricaded with slug pellets. In winter beans give way to Brussels sprouts (of which six different kinds are grown), and both purple and white sprouting broccoli.

An early plan of the walled garden at Felbrigg Hall. The old wall figs and pears have survived here for generations but there has been much new planting. The quadripod vines in the north border have become a feature of a number of National Trust gardens. The 'Norfolk Royal Russet' trees depicted so as to look like conifers are now doing well.

Cottagers kale and curly kale fill the winter beds with pretty purple and green rosettes and the crinkly Savoy cabbage 'January King' is grown – 'we got fed up with 'Ormskirk'.' American landcress supplies extra greens for winter salads and perpetual spinach lasts reasonably well into the winter. Broad beans such as 'Aqua Dulce' which can stand the winter are planted in autumn, and glass is put over them in January to coax an early crop. A little of the rhubarb is brought in for forcing and the rest is covered with straw which protects it and produces an early crop. After the mild winters of 1987/8 and 1988/9, the earliest sticks were being picked in January.

This is the month when the garlic cloves are put into pots in the greenhouse, to get a good start before they are planted out in March, when the onion sets also go in. Garlic does especially well if it is treated like this and planted more deeply than the onions. The Upton onions have always done so well, according to Mr Alan Philpott, that their quality was widely renowned. The varieties they now use are 'Ricardo' and 'Ailsa Craig' (the latter they raise from seed).

During the summer a full range of vegetables is grown, some of them varieties which have been grown for years, others trials of newer kinds. The French bean 'Sprite' has been dropped 'because it went off so soon' in favour of 'Prince'. Sugarpeas 'Garbon' and 'Oregon Pea' and different kinds of calabrese are also grown. In order to get a longer succession of crops, both F_1 hybrids (which come on faster) and non-F_1 varieties are grown. Up until now, the choice has remained fairly conservative, with asparagus beds, Florence fennel, Jerusalem artichokes and kohlrabi (sweet corn was dropped after the neighbourhood badgers developed a taste for it), but Miss Cook is keen to try a wider range of possibilities, as well as to enlarge the herb beds which are also contained within this garden. With its elegant surrounding borders and beautiful landscape, Upton opens the most exciting prospects for developing a large scale kitchen garden open to the public.

TRENGWAINTON in Cornwall has a rather unusual vegetable

garden made up of a series of raised beds facing west-south-west, built up at an angle of 45 degrees to get the maximum warmth from the spring sunshine. Lettuces, radishes and onions are sown under glass and transplanted into these sloping beds in early March. Shallots are planted in February. Mr Peter Horder, the Head Gardener here, would like to try more crops but the limitations of the labour available restrict the amount of time which can be devoted to the vegetables. Because of this a small range of plants which need relatively little attention is selected. Later on dwarf peas are grown, followed by marrows which 'romp all over the bed and look good'. De Caen anemones grown in the sloping beds also do well.

In winter the beds are dug over, starting at the top, and working evenly downwards to maintain the correct degree of slope. The beds consisting of 300-450mm/12-18in of soil over drainage stones, are very well drained and 'there is very little erosion, except in a downpour'. Mr Horder adds quantities of farmyard manure to his soil 'to improve the structure' and he also keeps working compost heaps and leafmould heaps in the vegetable garden as 'a cocktail for special plants'. Beds such as this were designed to give fresh vegetables for the occupants of the house at the very earliest opportunity. Elsewhere in the garden, potatoes, beans, peas and onions, carrots and several other kinds of vegetable and fruit are grown in the conventional manner.

At Trengwainton, as in many of the Trust properties, only part of the kitchen garden is kept in production – just enough to give visitors an impression of past practice. In most cases further ground is still available for productive use and should finances allow, perhaps through the means a volunteer support group or an educational venture, such as a practical demonstration centre, old kitchen gardens could be opened up more fully and skills passed on for the future.

The famous sloping beds at Trengwainton with their cargo of early beans, radish and young lettuce. Beds below are holding beds for tender plants which need shelter even in the mild Cornish winters.

At Styal in Cheshire there is a most interesting small working kitchen garden. The factory community at Styal, founded at the end of the eighteenth century, was given to the National Trust fifty years ago, and in the past few years the original cotton spinning mill and the APPRENTICE HOUSE have been restored by the local Quarry Bank Mill Trust and opened to the public as working museums.

One third of the work force in these early mills consisted of children, and many at Styal were housed a short walk from the mill. By the standards of the time the mill owners were enlightened and the children reasonably cared for. Fresh fruit and vegetables grown at the Apprentice House Garden made up a considerable part of their diet, and the children were expected to learn the useful skills of gardening and housekeeping – though when they found the time, after a twelve-hour working day, is something of a mystery.

The garden has been brought back into use over a period by the present gardener Mrs Patricia Brittan, who started at first with some model allotment plots but later restored the whole vegetable garden and orchard. Surviving plans of the one-and-a-half-acre site show vegetable and herb plots, an orchard and a drying green with hedges upon which clothes and linen were hung to dry. Records show some of the plants which were grown and the numbers of children who lived in the house. The first intake of apprentices took up residence in 1790 and by 1830, at the time that spinning machines and mechanical looms were introduced to the mill, the building housed eighty children. Detailed records survive from this period, so the restored house and garden are keyed as far as possible to this date.

Children from local schools (dressed in the costume of the time) now visit the Apprentice House for a day lived out as if

*Early days at the Apprentice House Garden
at Styal, when a small plot was worked as an allotment.
The present extended garden has restored the garden to its
nineteenth-century plan. The old apple and damson trees survive from
that time, while the fruit garden and Victorian
vegetable plot have been reconstructed.*

they were a new intake of apprentices. On the day I visited, a group of nine- and ten-year-olds were gathering herbs, weeding the rows of winter greens and digging up the first potatoes: a slightly diseased crop of 'Sefton Wonder' and some good 'Kerr's Pink'. Mrs Brittan enjoys these educational days, though 'the long skirts are a real bother when you're gardening'.

The garden is wholly organic and still in the process of reaching its ecological equilibrium and full fertility. Carrot fly takes a hard toll, although Mrs Brittan finds that 'planting carrots between rows of onions helps keep it at bay'. The HDRA (Henry Doubleday Research Association) have themselves been conducting experiments on this practice and found that a lot of onions (about four rows to one of carrots) are required to be effective.

Mrs Brittan is amused that some visitors are at first surprised by the garden: 'Not at all the kind of stately home garden, people generally expect when they see the National Trust symbol'. However, they soon become engrossed in this most unusual and interesting enterprise of historic reconstruction. There are numbers of famous fruits and vegetables which come from local origins. Altrincham, famed for its carrot, and Timperley of the famous 'Early Timperley' rhubarb are nearby villages. One of Mrs Brittan's best achievements is the restitution of a regional apple variety called 'Withington's Welter'. All the older people in the neighbourhood knew of it but none could point to an actual tree. Eventually Mrs Brittan tracked it down, had the fruits checked by the RHS at Wisley, and now a newly grafted tree (on vigorous MM106 stock) has taken its place in the replanted orchard alongside other varieties of the period such as 'Keswick Codlin' and 'Bismarck'. A remnant of the old orchard population survives, consisting of one old apple (which still defies identification) and several damsons.

Many historic varieties of gooseberry were developed in the northern counties of England, some of which survive in the National Collection at the University of Manchester's experimental grounds, attached to the Botany Department.

Young bushes were donated to the Apprentice House Garden by Manchester University. Mrs Brittan carefully chose several known to thrive locally, including 'King of Trumps', 'London', 'Hero of the Nile', 'Catherina' and the ubiquitous 'Careless', all varieties which won prizes in one of the nineteenth-century gooseberry shows at neighbouring Wilmslow.

Mrs Brittan assembled her vegetable collection by ordering from catalogues which specialized in old or unusual vegetables, especially Heritage Seeds from the HDRA and Boyce of Cambridge. The garden is sandstone overlaid with clay – 'not ideal for growing prize-size 'Altrincham' carrots, which are long bodied – but many of the other varieties do surprisingly well': 'China Rose' winter radish, 'Ragged Jack' kale, the onion 'Robinson's Mammoth' and lettuce 'Bath Cos' are all varieties Mrs Brittan rates as very good. She is pragmatic about her historic fruit and vegetables. 'We're not trying to prove old is best,' she says, commenting that she can see 'why some things have gone out of fashion'. She does not romanticize a variety simply because it is old, but gives praise where it is due. She approves of the old radish 'Woods Early Frame' but is disdainful about the lettuce 'Loos Tennis Ball.' She explains, 'In the first year I thought it was me, but after three I stopped growing it any more. It goes to seed as soon as you look at it.'

Winter vegetables such as this 'Brown Winter Radish', the more oblong red 'China Rose' or the large white 'Japanese Winter Radish' are making a welcome return to gardens. Pods of winter radish left to run to seed in spring make a spicy addition to early salads.

There was difficulty with historic peas. 'Carlin' peas (on the EEC proscribed list) figure no longer in anybody's catalogue and nobody seemed to have seed. By an odd chance Mrs Brittan came across them 'sold for pease pudding' in a health shop and found that they grew well. 'Prince Albert' peas appeared to have been 'totally lost from this country', but Lawrence Hills of the HDRA managed to get a few in America and donated some to the Apprentice House. All seemed set fair when mice got into the rows and ate all the precious seed peas, leaving but two unconsumed. Mrs Brittan nurtured these two, saved the seed and in 1988 produced a row of twenty (with some seed peas carefully put by, in case of disaster).

Mrs Brittan acts as 'seed guardian', growing on a few rare varieties to produce seed which is sent back to the HDRA. In addition to 'Prince Albert' peas, seed is saved from the beetroot 'Cook's Delight', (which Mrs Brittan rates 'a very good beetroot, unusual because it is cylindrical in shape'), and from several other vegetables. Those plants selected for seed are then grown in isolation from other varieties (where cross pollination is a problem) so that the seed comes completely true.

The bothy at Calke Abbey with its flagged and brick floor, still furnished with seed cabinet,
gardener's desk, hessian sacking and binder twine. Several Trust gardens retain old outbuildings such as this,
as functional now as in the past – though the old account books read a little differently from modern ones.

One of the most exciting new developments in National Trust Gardens is the restoration of a kitchen garden at CALKE ABBEY in Derbyshire. This is taking place not on the site of the original eighteenth-century kitchen garden, which was thought to be too large, but on that of the old physic garden,

about a quarter the size. Calke Abbey, the home of the Harpur Crewe family, is a large estate with fine landscapes, park and gardens. The present object is to make a new kitchen garden using fruit trees and soft fruits, vegetables and herbs in keeping with the period of the house.

*Above: The spikey grey-green foliage of
globe artichokes, as attractive as acanthus, at Upton House.
Opposite: An attractive scene in the garden at
West Green in summer, dominated by the tall globe-headed
angelica and mature rhubarb leaves, with a line of 'chimney
pot' forcing jars leading the eye to the ornamental
fruit cages in the distance.*

It is known that the kitchen garden of the past was a mixture of the practical and ornamental and must have looked very attractive. The 65m/71yd tunnel at the eastern end of the pleasure ground that led underground to the walled garden (thus keeping it entirely separate from the rest of the garden complex) still exists but has not yet been repaired and opened up. Likewise it is hoped that the beautiful but ruined orangery will be restored in due course, along with most of the other extensive glass houses.

Work on the remaking of the kitchen garden began in 1987, under the imaginative leadership of Head Gardener Mr Stephen Biggins, with clearing, remaking paths and beds. Fruits such as the 'Lloyd George' and 'Yellow Antwerp' raspberries, 'Royal Sovereign' strawberry, 'Goliath' and 'Boskoop Giant' black currants, and 'White Dutch' currant, 'Wilson's Longbunch' and 'Fay's Prolific' red currants were introduced. Notes on the National Collection of gooseberries were consulted before 'Whitesmith', 'Keepsake' and 'Lancer' were selected for the garden. The Northern Horticultural Society's gardeners at Harlow Carr Gardens in Harrogate were consulted over rhubarbs (of which they hold the National Collection).

An asparagus bed has been established and a small rose bed converted to a bed of globe artichokes. Other large vegetables such as cardoons and Jerusalem artichokes also have their own separate beds. One of the many glasshouses will be retained in use as a tomato house, and another used for cucumbers. The dilapidated frames are to be restored gradually, over a period, re-using the old glass panes with curved ends. Only parts of the original wall from the old orchard remain and these are to be conserved as historically important artefacts. A few trees of pear 'Barland' and 'Early Rivers' cherry are being planted in this old orchard area of the pleasure ground along with a larger number of ornamentals. Other fruit trees such as medlar, black mulberry and quince are planned for the old walled garden along with a double row of cobnuts, but the new orchard will be planted to the east of the physic garden.

THE   KITCHEN   GARDEN

FLOWERS AND EXOTIC FRUIT

The gardeners of the great houses of the past were expected as part of their everyday duties to supply the family (and often members of the family living elsewhere) with a wide range of produce. This involved not only the regular kitchen garden crops of seasonal fruit and vegetables, but special fruits produced under glass, vegetables forced out of season, and cut flowers and potted plants to decorate the house. During seasonal festivities and when large house parties were being entertained, this put considerable strain upon the gardeners, especially during the winter, but generally the work fell into a seasonal routine which was discussed with the head gardener well in advance of requirements.

Few private houses now survive on these lines and it is fortunate that just before the owner Lady Catherine Macdonald-Buchanan died in 1987 a journal of activities in the garden at Cottesbrooke in Northamptonshire was written and illustrated with drawings and photographs. This shows clearly the expectations of an employer (in this case one who had actually lived during the Victorian period) translated into twentieth-century practice by a very able and responsive Head Gardener, Mr Doug Brereton, and his staff.

A wide variety of vegetables, fruit and flowers, including glass-house produce, was grown throughout the year, and sent to the house in daily consignments, the precise kinds and quantities decided in collaboration with the cook. At Christmas, parcels of fruit and vegetable produce were carefully packed into hampers and sent off to absent members of the family. Up until only a few years ago, the flowers produced for the house included chrysanthemums, orchids, nerines, freesias, geraniums and carnations raised in the extensive and beautifully ordered glasshouses.

Above: Lemons in fruit in the Saltram orangery in Devon, continuing a long tradition of growing citrus fruits, attractive both in blossom and fruit for much of the year.

Opposite: A brilliant scene at Peckover House, looking through an arch of Japanese quince (Chaenomeles) to the well-kept conservatory with its geranium and fuchsia border.

*Melon-growing mounted to a passion during the eighteenth century, among gentleman
gardeners who grew them in hot beds, carefully regulating heat, light and humidity. This one, beginning to
ripen in the August heat, is under glass at Barrington Court.*

Hyacinths, narcissi, cyclamen and cinerarias were used extensively as pot plants. Melons, peaches, grapes and figs were produced in a special range of glasshouses. It was all expensive and time-consuming, but the head gardener, combining modern knowledge and old skills, managed to conform to the standards and practices of the past, with three full-time gardeners and some part-time help: far fewer staff than would have been allocated him a hundred years ago.

For obvious reasons, gardeners are not trained in such things nowadays, and it is only an older generation who have been through a long apprenticeship in an estate garden who have the knowledge and skills necessary to order such a demanding regime. Few National Trust gardens have any direct responsibility towards supplying the needs of the old family, although some, such as HARDWICK and FELBRIGG, do still grow flowers specifically for decorating the house. Where fruit and vegetables are grown as part of the garden scheme, the administrator or curator and the gardeners themselves are often beneficiaries, as at MOSELEY OLD HALL, TINTINHULL and TRENGWAINTON. In a minority of cases, the head gardener is also responsible to the family for certain items, as at ASCOTT where hot-house plants and fruit are supplied in season to the Rothschilds.

The Victorian gardens and grounds at Ascott, near Leighton Buzzard in Buckinghamshire, were given to the National Trust in 1950 by Mr and Mrs de Rothschild. The gardeners there are responsible to the Trust in matters pertaining to the 39 acres (15.5 hectares) of garden, but they also serve the house with a regular supply of foliage and flowering plants which are used for decoration.

There are ornamental palms such as kentias (*Howeia forsteriana*), which originates from Lord Howe Island off Australia but which has acclimatized well to conservatory life. There are also chamaedoreas (*Chamaedorea elegans*), members of a large Amazonian genus which have also been adopted for indoor and glasshouse cultivation because they are tolerant of dim light, so long as they are kept fairly humid. Known as parlour palms, the fronds are made up of

Grapes, grown successfully under glass for centuries, are still a feature of many country house conservatories and orangeries. These are at The Courts in Wiltshire.

pairs of dark green, leathery, tapering leaflets. They can be propagated by seed in spring (germinating at a constant 20–24°C/68-75°F).

Ferns are also cultivated in the conservatories as foliage plants in their own right, or to make a background to bright flowers. The well-known maidenhairs (*Adiantum* spp.), beautiful but fragile, appreciate the humid conditions (and don't thrive as house plants in dry, centrally heated rooms), but there are several more tolerant types such as the asparagus fern: the feathery *Asparagus setaceus* (also known as *A. plumosus*) and the appropriately named foxtail fern *Asparagus densiflorus* 'Myers' (often sold labelled as *Asparagus meyeri*).

Scented-leaf geraniums and the dainty sweetly perfumed jasmine (*Jasminum polyanthum*) present few cultivation problems, but gardenias, grown for their powerful fragrance, demand knowledge, skill and precise temperature control. They need a night-time temperature which never drops below 16°C/60°F with day temperatures about 5.5°C/10°F higher in order for flowerbuds to form, and steady temperature levels and watering for the buds not to fall off. The plants are raised in the conservatories, going up to the house at their peak, and returning to be nursed back into condition after their stint as house plants.

The gardeners also tend a range of orchids which spend the showiest periods of their life at the house. The main accent is on cymbidiums including standard and miniature forms of a dozen or named varieties, but they also grow odontoglossums, hybrid cultivars called vuylstekearas, and the beautiful moth orchids (*Phalaenopsis*), the new cultivars of which are probably the ones best suited to domestic life.

Other National Trust properties also grow pot plants as a specific crop. At HARDWICK, for example, they are raised in the traditional way in a greenhouse which is specially set aside for their production, while at ACORN BANK Mr Braithwaite is exceptionally pleased with his exotic red cherry guava (*Psidium littorale*), an elegant plant with green leaves with burnished red tips.

The moth orchid (*Phalaenopsis*) needs humidity as a house plant: set the plant pots on an upturned plant saucer firmed into the damp gravel (not in direct sun).

The flowering stem carries 6-8 flowers which bloom over a period of many weeks. When only two flowers are left, the stem should be cut above the top node (lump on the stem) and below the point where the first flower appeared. Over a period of 14-16 weeks, the node will swell and form a new flowering spike.

At Hardwick, all of the flowers used in the Hall are grown in the garden and are determined by the season. The lily of the valley 'Hardwick Hall' is an elegant cut flower with its cream-edged leaf. Other specialities include several scabious (Hardwick holds the National Collection of *Scabiosa caucasica*). Penstemons, campanulas, lupins, roses and delphiniums of different sorts make the summer gay. Later they are followed by *Cleome, Chrysanthemum maximum, Lavatera* and many others.

At FELBRIGG HALL a few rows of plants for cutting provide a skirt around the area set aside for vegetables and soft fruit. Mrs Gillian Hart, a tenant at Felbrigg who kindly does the service of collecting and arranging the flowers, has observed that unusual plants always draw the attention of the visitors. The green (Viridis) tulips, small gladioli, abutilons (*A. megapotamicum* and *A. thompsonii*) always receive comment, to the extent that the guides ask to be briefed on new floral arrangements. Overall, Mrs Hart looks for colours which 'blend with the soft tones of the furnishings in the house', the best colours being 'soft reds, all pinks, soft oranges, apricot, lemon yellow, cream and a good deal of white'. She is specific about the link between the house and garden, 'using the flower arrangements in the house to make people look more closely at what is grown in the garden'. She particularly favours well-shaped flowers such as lilies, tulips and irises in an arrangement, with scented plants such as sweet peas for bedrooms.

Helenium, lady's mantle (*Alchemilla mollis*) and *Leucanthemum maximum*, the big Shasta daisy, are good cutting plants which are regularly used, all producing good blooms through the summer and into early autumn. Statuesque plants such as cardoon, acanthus (*Acanthus mollis latifolius* and *A. spinosus*) and the blue-green globe thistle (*Echinops ritro*) are valuable in flower arrangements, and beautiful cut flower blooms including the autumn Japanese anemone (*Anemone × hybrida*) and the Californian tree poppy (*Romneya coulteri*) are also sought after. More unusual subjects are *Salvia turkestanica* and an uncommon kind of Jacob's ladder called *Polemonium foliosissimum* as well as the autumn Michaelmas daisies (*Aster × frikartii*) which flower well into September and October.

Rhizomes and bulbs which are used include lilies – the white Madonna (*Lilium candidum*) and *L. regale*, the yellow *Lilium testaceum*, and belladonna lily (*Amaryllis belladonna*); crown imperial (*Fritillaria imperialis*) and Solomon's seal (*Polygonatum × hybridum*). Moving from spring into summer there are narcissus cultivars, chincherinchee (*Ornithogalum thyrsoides*) and lily of the valley (*Convallaria majalis*), and in the autumn the showy nerines (*Nerine bowdenii*) brighten the display. These are 'mainstay plants', which are combined with other flowers and pieces of flowering shrubs and trees.

One of the famous ancient fuchsias, huge, gnarled and liberally hung with blooms, in the conservatory at Wallington.

PRIORWOOD GARDENS, in Melrose in the Borders, which is under the charge of The National Trust for Scotland, specializes in growing a wide variety of everlasting flowers as well as herbaceous perennials and annuals which are suitable for drying. Over seven hundred different kinds are now cultivated for this purpose, including peonies, cornflowers, zinnias and miniature roses. The leaves and blooms are harvested by volunteers and sold in The National Trust Flower Shop.

Priorwood labels all its plants and produces useful leaflets which give details of almost everything grown in the different shrub borders, herbaceous borders, patio garden, rose and herb garden. The part of the plant which is picked for drying is itemized and the preferred method for preserving them indicated. Other informational leaflets explain the different drying techniques and ways of arranging, so a complete picture of the process is given.

Some of the other gardens are beginning to put to use the plants they grow. At MOSELEY OLD HALL, ripe pears are bagged and sold to visitors, and when parties of school children come to experience life as it was lived in the seventeenth century, they find themselves not simply baking and embroidering but making lavender bags and pot pourri from the lavender, herbs and flowers. All the produce from the APPRENTICE HOUSE GARDEN at Styal is also used, some of it by visiting children. Mr Peter Horder at TRENGWAINTON markets a few flowers as a commercial crop: 'Kaffir lilies (*Schizostylis coccinea*) and alstroemerias – things that don't take too much labour'. ARCHAMORE GARDENS on the beautiful island of Gigha, where the famous collection of rhododendrons and tender trees and shrubs is in the care of the National Trust for Scotland, now has a thriving propagation and nursery business run by the Head Gardener Mr George Hall, using three poly-tunnels.

Several gardens have an area set aside for plant sales, but BLICKLING HALL in Norfolk has entered into association with the nursery firm Bressingham Gardens, who have undertaken to propagate several of the Blickling specialities for sale to the public as the 'Blickling Collection'. It is possible that other gardens will also pursue this idea and that other exciting plants from National Trust gardens will find their way to a wider public.

Glasshouses have an important role in growing and overwintering plants for the National Trust. Some of the properties are endowed with beautiful and architecturally important orangeries and conservatories as well as practical glasshouses. A passion for building conservatories ran high in the late nineteenth century, and now, about a hundred years later, it is once again the fastest growing section of the horticultural market. Building the conservatory is nearly always a traumatic business, but once it is in place, the building pains are quickly forgotten and the business in hand becomes how to furnish and plant it. Unfortunately, the style of manufacture sometimes precludes successful conservatory gardening without substantial modification.

*Above: A corner of the hard-working glasshouse
at Hope End, with a nectarine trained up the supports.
All the seedlings and cuttings are raised here, to be planted
out into the kitchen garden or the courtyards.
Opposite: Peonies hanging up to dry at Priorwood
in Melrose. The arrangements made by the staff at this National
Trust for Scotland garden are remarkable for the perfection
of the flowers and the beauty and form of the display.*

Previous page: The Orangery, adorned with wisterias, which was built at Hanbury Hall about 1732, when it was part of an elaborate formal garden hardly anything of which now remains.

Citrus trees, especially certain species such as the Calamondin orange, make excellent conservatory or greenhouse plants requiring only a temperature of about 50-60°F/10-15°C in winter. The container should be crocked at the bottom and given a layer of gravel to ensure good drainage. It needs full sun and benefits from a period out of doors in summer.

Briefly, a conservatory in which plants and people can enjoy life should have opening windows in the roof (to allow for ventilation and egress for flies). There should also be some shade, either natural or through blinds, as temperatures can get up to tropical heights as early in the year as February in an unheated conservatory. Lastly, the selection of plants which can be grown will depend very much upon the aspect of the building and whether, or how much, it can be heated during the winter time.

Gardeners who are thinking of building a conservatory could profit from visits to glasshouses, orangeries and conservatories at several of the National Trust properties. Most will, of course, be grander than the average home conservatory, but interesting lessons can be drawn about the style of design and operation – and the plants which can be grown within them, with the minimum of heating and labour.

Owing to the cost of heating, most of the National Trust glasshouses and orangeries are maintained as cool conservatories – that is, frost-free with an ambient winter temperature not falling below 5–7°C/40-45°F. This means that although there are oranges to be found – at TATTON PARK, for example, where the trees are thought to be about two hundred years old – the temperature is not now adequate to ripen them and the once-renowned oranges remain unsweetened.

DUNSTER CASTLE, near Minehead, enjoys the relatively gentle climate of the north Somerset coast which enables glasshouse plants such as the arum lily and mimosa (*Acacia dealbata*) to thrive out of doors. The sunny terrace immediately below the castle is home for a venerable lemon tree which the Head Gardener Mr Michael Marshall assesses at well over a hundred years old. Mr Graham Stuart Thomas discovered a reference to a lemon which was 'well-established in 1842' when it was mentioned in Loudon's *Gardener's Magazine*, but Mr Marshall thinks it doubtful that

The Orangery at Peckover House, colourful with pots of cineraria and calceolaria crowding the shelves. Their well-grown orange trees with shiny leaves and bright fruit are exceptional. The attractiveness of this glass house owes much to its decorative cast iron and colourfully patterned tiled floor.

it is the same one. The tree grows on the north-east wall of the castle, with another thought to be about eighty years old, and both bear fruit all the year round. It has clearly become something of a custom to have citrus trees at Dunster. They have always had some protection during the winter time – though no heat even in the severest weather. When the old shelter collapsed in 1981, the National Trust had a new vertical cold frame made with 'three sets of double doors and top and bottom light – and with extra thick glass. During fine weather these remain permanently open.' There is also a small collection of other citrus fruits which stand along the south terrace in a row of tubs during the summer and are stored in a small conservatory at the west end of the terrace during the winter.

One can also find old orange trees at TATTON PARK and at PECKOVER HOUSE, in Wisbech, Cambridgeshire, where the orangery standing in a Victorian garden contains trees 'which are reputedly over three hundred years old'. They were, according to a record written about 1898, at least two hundred years old when they were 'purchased at a famous sale at Hagbeach Hall'.

At SALTRAM, near Plympton in Devon, the orangery, damaged by fire in 1932, was repaired by the National Trust in 1961. Its original plants, oranges and lemons purchased in 1811, used to be taken under cover in the orangery on Tavistock Goose Fair Day (held on the second Wednesday in October) and they were brought outside on 29 May (Oak Apple Day) each year, even when some of them had grown to 3.6m/12ft. Those old trees are gone now, but their replacements which were imported from Spain and Portugal, having got used to their new nationality, are treated in the same way – except that they are now transported to their summer quarters in the orange grove by modern-day tractor.

The imposing Orangery at Saltram, basking behind its stately columns. Originally built in 1771, it was destroyed by fire in 1932. It was reconstructed by the Trust in 1961.

At FELBRIGG, the orangery is used to grow camellias. Protected from the harsh weather that can bring in an East Anglian spring, the blooms last much longer than they would outside. At the base of the camellias there are tender ferns such as *Woodwardia radicans*, *Polystichum tsus-simense* and *Adiantum pedatum*, providing a softly contrasting foliage to that of the dark glossy camellias. In the conservatory at WALLINGTON, fuchsias are a special feature. Some of these are very old with huge tree-like trunks. A pale lavender-coloured heliotrope is another special plant grown in this interesting conservatory.

CLUMBER PARK in Nottinghamshire also has extensive glasshouses, and their long-galleried conservatory has recently been beautifully restored and replanted with wall fruit in the form of figs, peaches and nectarines and grapes. (It also houses a most interesting exhibition of garden tools.) English glasshouse grapes (many of them raised at Chilwell, near Clumber) played an important role in the late Victorian and early twentieth-century gardens. One of the best early grapes, 'Foster's Seedling' (a hybrid between 'Black Morocco' and 'Sweetwater'), was raised at BENINGBROUGH HALL *circa* 1835 by Mr Foster, gardener to Lord Downe. The same parentage produced another famous grape, 'Lady Downe's Seedling' for Mr Foster, this one ripening late in the season. Both kinds are still grown at Beningbrough.

Some of the money raised by the CALKE ABBEY appeal is destined toward the restoration and repair of some of the extensive glasshouses. The most elegant is the eighteenth-century orangery which ran the length of the old kitchen garden. It must have been very grand, with its semi-circular headed sash windows, decorative plasterwork and glass dome. It housed several citrus trees and a collection of pelargoniums, but over the last three or four decades, it has fallen into dereliction. According to the Trust's report in 1987, 'The glass dome has collapsed and the window frames are broken', but – maybe a signal of hope – the Trust also notes that 'It houses a solitary palm, struggling for survival against the British climate'.

PRODUCTIVE GARDENS OF THE NATIONAL TRUST

Acorn Bank Garden, *Temple Sowerby, near Penrith, Cumbria (07683) 61281*
Large herb garden and orchards.

Apprentice House Garden, *see*
Quarry Bank Mill

Bateman's, *Burwash, Etchingham, Sussex (0435) 882302*
Trained pear alley.

Beningbrough Hall, *Shipton-by-Beningbrough, York, North Yorkshire (0904) 470666*
Trained fruit trees.

Barrington Court, *near Ilminster, Somerset (0460) 40610/52242*
Excellent displays of fruit and vegetables.

Berrington Hall, *near Leominster, Hereford and Worcester (0568) 5721*
Local apple collection.

Blickling Hall, *Blickling, Norfolk (0263) 733084*
Home of the Blickling Pear.

Calke Abbey, *Ticknall, Derbyshire (0332) 863822*
Kitchen gardens in process of restoration.

Canons Ashby House, *Canons Ashby, Daventry, Northamptonshire (0327) 860044*
Fruit collection.

Clumber Park, *Worksop, Nottinghamshire (0909) 476592*
Good glasshouses with exotic fruits, vegetable borders, tool collection.

Cotehele, *St Dominic, near Saltash, Cornwall (0579) 50434*
Interesting fruit collection of local varieties.

Dunster Castle, *Dunster, near Minehead, Somerset (0643) 821314*
Famous Dunster lemon and other citrus fruits on the terrace.

Erddig, *near Wrexham, Clwyd (0978) 355314*
Orchard, trained fruit, fruit collection.

Felbrigg Hall, *Norwich, Norfolk (026 375) 444*
Small orchard, wall fruit, some vegetables, soft fruit and flowers for cutting within the walled garden.

Fenton House, *Windmill Hill, Hampstead, London 01 435 3471*
Wall trained fruit. Garden under restoration beginning 1989.

Glendurgan Garden, *Helford River, Mawnan Smith, near Falmouth, Cornwall (0208) 4821*
Cornish varieties of apple in new orchard.

Greys Court, *Rotherfield Greys, Henley-on-Thames, Oxfordshire (049 17) 529*
Kitchen garden and orchard.

Gunby Hall, *Gunby, near Spilsby, Lincolnshire*
Walled kitchen garden/potager.

Hardwick Hall, *Doe Lea, Chesterfield, Derbyshire (0246) 850430*
Famous herb garden.

Lytes Cary Manor, *Charlton Mackrell, Somerton, Somerset*
Herb garden.

Moseley Old Hall, *Moseley Old Hall Lane, Fordhouses, Wolverhampton, Staffordshire (0902) 782808*
Formal herb garden. Nut trees and fruit.

Nunnington Hall, *Nunnington, York (043 95) 283*
Orchard including collection of local fruit.

Peckover House, *North Brink, Wisbech, Cambridgeshire (0945) 583463*
Orangery.

Powis Castle, *Welshpool, Powys (0938) 4336*
Trained forms of fruit.

Quarry Bank Mill, Apprentice House Garden, *Styal, Wilmslow, Cheshire (0625) 527468*
Victorian fruit and vegetable kitchen garden.

Saltram, *Plympton, Plymouth, Devon (0752) 336546*
Orange and lemon trees in the orangery.

Scotney Castle, *Lamberhurst, Tunbridge Wells, Kent (0892) 890651*
Herb garden.

Sissinghurst Castle Garden, *Sissinghurst, near Cranbrook, Kent (0580) 712850*
Famous herb garden, wall fruit.

Tintinhull House, *Tintinhull, near Yeovil, Somerset (0747) 840224*
Kitchen garden and adjacent orchard/arboretum (not open to the public).

Trengwainton Garden, *near Penzance, Cornwall*
(0736) 63021
Sloping early vegetable beds.

Upton House, *Banbury, Oxfordshire (029 587) 266*
Large, impressive kitchen garden.

Wallington, *Cambo, Morpeth, Northumberland*
(067 074) 283
Conservatory.

Westbury Court Garden, *Westbury-on-Severn,*
Gloucestershire (045 276) 461
Long fruit wall with historic apple, pear and plum
espaliers. Small walled rose/herb garden.

West Green House, *Hartley Wintney, Basingstoke,*
Hampshire (0252) 2332
Kitchen garden/potager; fruit trees; ornamental
fruit cages.

Wightwick Manor, *Wightwick Bank,*
Wolverhampton (0902) 761108
The 'Tetton Hall' pear, mulberry and medlar.

Wimpole Hall, *Arrington, Royston, Hertfordshire*
(0223) 207257
Walnut collection.

NATIONAL TRUST FOR SCOTLAND

Kellie Castle and Garden, *Pittenweem, Fife*
(08338) 271
Fruit and vegetables grown among flowers.

Pitmedden Garden, *Ellon, Aberdeenshire*
(065 13) 2352
Herb garden, fruit and vegetables.

Priorwood Garden, *Melrose, Roxburghshire*
(089682) 2965
Orchard; herb and flower garden; plants used for
drying.

Threave Garden, *Castle Douglas, Kirkcudbrightshire*
(0556) 2575
Pear collection; walled garden with fruit trees and
soft fruit; some vegetables.

SELECTED READING

Baker, Harry. *The Fruit Garden Displayed.* Cassell Ltd/ RHS, 1986.

Baker, Harry. *Fruit.* Mitchell Beazley/ RHS 1980.

Bunyard, E. A. *A Handbook of Fruits (Apples and Pears).* John Murray 1920.

Bunyard, E. A. *A Handbook of Fruits (Stone and Bush fruits, Nuts etc).* John Murray 1925.

Bunyard, E. A. *An Anatomy of Fruit.* Chatto and Windus 1933.

Campbell, Susan and Palmer, Hue. *Cottesbroke.* Century Hutchinson 1987.

Clarke, Ethne. *The Art of the Kitchen Garden.* Michael Joseph 1988.

Greenoak, Francesca. *Forgotten Fruit.* Deutsch 1983.

Grubb, N. H. *Cherries.* Crosby Lockwood & Son 1949.

Hamilton, Geoff. *Successful Organic Gardening.* Dorling Kindersley 1987.

Hills, Lawrence. *The Good Fruit Guide.* HDRA. The National Centre for Organic Gardening 1984.

Hills, Lawrence. *Vegetable Pest and Disease Control the Organic Way.* HDRA. The National Centre for Organic Gardening 1983.

Hills, Lawrence. *Fruit Pest and Disease Control The Organic Way.* HDRA. The National Centre for Organic Gardening 1983.

Hogg, Robert. *The Fruit Manual* 5th ed. 1884.

Larkcom, Joy. *Salads The Year Round.* Hamlyn 1980.

Larkcom, Joy. *The Salad Garden.* Windward 1984.

Larkcom, Joy. *Vegetables from Small Gardens* (revised edition). Faber 1986.

Luckwill, L. C. & Pollard, A. *Perry Pears.* University of Bristol 1963.

Pears, Pauline. *Raised Bed Gardening The Organic Way.* HDRA. The Centre for Organic Gardening 1983.

Taylor, H. V. *The Apples of England.* Crosby Lockwood & Son 1948.

Taylor, H. V. *The Plums of England.* Crosby Lockwood & Son 1949.

USEFUL ADDRESSES

Chris Bowers and Sons, *Whispering Trees Nursery, Wimbotsham, Norfolk (0366) 388752*
Wide selection of fruit.

Deacon's Nursery, *Godshill, Isle of Wight (098 389) 750/778*
Good choice of apples, pears and plums, including trained forms.

Family Trees, *Summerlands, Curdridge, Botley, Southampton (0489) 26680*
Several varieties grafted on one tree (for smaller gardens).

Highfield Nurseries, *Western Forestry Co. Ltd, Whitminster, Gloucester (0452) 740266*
Good selection of trained forms.

Ken Muir, *Honeypot Farm, Rectory Road, Weeley Heath, Clacton-on-Sea, Essex (0255) 830181*
Good soft fruit catalogue list.

New Tree Nurseries, *2 Nunnery Road, Canterbury, Kent (0227) 61209*

Read's Nursery, *Hales Hall, Loddon, Norfolk (0508) 46395*

R V Roger Ltd, *The Nurseries, Pickering, North Yorkshire (0751) 72226*
Good all round catalogue list, excellent gooseberries.

Scotts Nurseries (Merriott) Ltd, *Merriott, Somerset (0460) 72306*
Probably the most comprehensive list of apples, pears, plums and other top fruit.

NOTE: Many of the catalogues have pollination tables or some indication of which plants can be grown together. Full explanations or charts are also given in *The Good Fruit Guide, Fruit* and *The Fruit Garden Displayed* (see Selected Reading, above).

NCCPG FRUIT REGISTER

S.F. Baldock, *Costrels, Eton Bishop, Hereford HR2 9QW*
Mr Baldock is fruit collator for the NCCPG and is compiling a list of English apples introduced prior to 1900. The information required is as follows: the names and numbers of each variety in groups, collections or as individual trees; their approximate size; the location. If local names only are known, please give these with a brief description of the fruit and its season of ripening.

OPEN DAYS

Look out for orchard open days such as the one at:
Blackmoor Fruit Nurseries, *Blackmoor, Liss, Hampshire (04203) 3576*

Try the different fruits for taste. They are usually advertised in the local press and radio.

The Royal Horticultural Society, *Vincent Square, Westminster, London SW1P 2PE (01) 834 4333*
The RHS has regular shows which feature fruit and vegetables at its Exhibition Halls in Vincent Square. Details can be obtained from the RHS at the above address.

FRUIT TRIALS AND DEMONSTRATIONS

Harlow Carr Botanical Gardens, *(The Northern Horticultural Society), Crag Lane, Harrogate, North Yorkshire HG3 1QB*
Apple trees, vegetable plots (including deep beds), soft fruit, National Collection of rhubarb. Regular demonstrations of gardening techniques.

HDRA (Henry Doubleday Research Association), *National Centre for Organic Gardening, Ryton-on-Dunsmore, Coventry CV8 3LG*
Plots of fruit trees on different stocks; cordons; soft fruit; unusual vegetables; allotment gardening; disease control without pesticides.

RHS Garden, *Wisley, Woking, Surrey GU23 6QB*
Extensive model plots of fruit and vegetables. Regular demonstrations of growing, maintenance and pruning.

INDEX

Note: figures in **bold** refer to
illustrations.

ACKNOWLEDGEMENTS

Credit first and especially must go to the head gardeners and some of the custodians, tenants and administrators of the National Trust properties, who, without complaint or resentment, generously guided me around their gardens and showed me their specialities, confided problems and answered the numerous questions I put to them. I owe a great debt to each of those whom I consulted and I wish here to thank them all. I should also like to express my gratitude to Penelope Hobhouse for asking me to take part in this series, and to the team at Pavilion who have brought this book to publication.

The publishers wish to thank the National Trust and its photographers for their kind permission to reproduce the following photographs:

John Bethell: pp. 47, 54, 97; **Neil Cambell Sharp**: pp. 21, 27, 32, 44, 46, 60, 62, 63, 68, 71, 72, 84, 87, 88, 89; **Nick Carter**: pp. 57, 58; **Eric Crichton**: pp. 38, 45; **Ray Hallett**: p. 86; **Angelo Hornak**: pp. 19, 94/5; **Horst Kolo**: p. 29; **Anthony Lambert**: p. 77; **Rob Matheson**: pp. 23, 28 (top and bottom), 44; **Nick Meers**: pp. 15, 98; **Phil Nixon**: p. 91; **Glyn Satterley**: p. 92; **Michael Warren**: p. 43; **Mike Williams**: pp. 16, 20, 24, 34, 48, 51, 65, 66, 80.

The Publishers wish to thank the following for their kind permission to reproduce the following photographs:

Francesca Greenoak: pp. 25, 64; **Tony Lord**: pp. 11, 17, 49, 56, 74/5, 83, 85; **Andrew Lawson**: p. 67; *Woman and Home*/Jacqui Hurst: pp. 8, 69, 93.

NOTES